SUSTAINABLE CITIES IN EUROPE

Worldwide, urbanization is steadily increasing, yet many modern cities are becoming less and less able to accommodate the growth in their population. Congestion, pollution, low-quality housing, social fragmentation, noise, crime and inadequate social services all contribute to a declining quality of urban life. Planners and policy makers are battling to alleviate the problems with a variety of urban renewal initiatives, and energy–environmental policies have become central to their quest for urban sustainability.

Sustainable Cities in Europe gives a comprehensive introduction to the available urban energy and environmental policies. Drawing on a detailed analysis of the CITIES programme of the Commission of the European Communities, the book includes detailed case studies of European cities which are devising and implementing alternative strategies for sustainable growth and development. The cities discussed include:

● Amsterdam ● Besançon ● Bragança ● Cadiz ● Dublin ● Esch/Alzette ● Gent ● Mannheim ● Newcastle ● Odense ● Thessaloniki ● Turin

The policy discussions and case studies in this book will be invaluable for all those professionally or academically involved in the pressing issue of city planning development.

Peter Nijkamp is Professor in Regional, Urban and Environmental Economics at Free University, Amsterdam. Author of numerous books, he is a world authority on environmental economics and urban policy. Adriaan Perrels is head of the research department of the Energy Studies Centre in Petten, The Netherlands. He has worked extensively in the field of energy planning and electricity load management.

SUSTAINABLE CITIES IN EUROPE

A Comparative Analysis of Urban
Energy—Environmental Policies

PETER NIJKAMP &
ADRIAAN PERRELS

EARTHSCAN

Earthscan Publications Ltd, London

First published in the UK in 1994 by
Earthscan Publications Limited
120 Pentonville Road, London N1 9JN

ISBN: 1 85383 203 0

Typeset by Meta Publishing Services, London
Printed and bound in Great Britain by
Biddles Ltd, Guildford and King's Lynn

Earthscan Publications is an editorially independent subsidiary of Kogan
Page Limited and publishes in association with the International Institute
for Environment and Development and the World Wide Fund for Nature.

CONTENTS

List of Illustrations

FIGURES

TABLES

PREFACE

The city is our home. In most cases it is the place where we find work, shelter and services. It is therefore no surprise that the urbanization rate shows a steady increase all over the world. At the same time however, it has to be recognized that most modern cities are not fulfilling their tasks in a satisfactory manner. The negative externalities show an alarming growth rate, resulting in increasing threats to cities in both the developed and the developing world. Congestion, pollution, crime, noise, poor quality housing, social segmentation and numerous other factors contribute to a declining quality of life in urban society.

This awareness has generated great concern, but also new initiatives to rejuvenate the city. Gentrification, urban renewal and urban environmental policy have become important responses aimed at generating or maintaining a liveable city characterized by environmental sustainability in a broad sense. As a result, urban energy–environmental policies have become a focal point of policy interest.

This book aims to bring together experiences from various European cities aiming at developing a sustainable development for their urban territory. It is taken for granted that – apart from generic environmental policy measures which will have to be implemented anyway – the city is the place *par excellence* where an intensified urban energy policy may bring about a wide variety of favourable environmental impacts. This may lead to a drastic improvement of environmental quality in European cities and hence may favour the rise of sustainable cities in Europe.

The studies and documents underlying this volume were generated as part of the so-called CITIES programme of the Commission of the European Communities (Directorate General Energy) with the aim to offer interesting learning examples to other cities in Europe. The authors wish to thank the Commission for its support. In compiling this book the authors also wish to recognize the support given by numerous experts all over Europe, in particular Else Berndsen, Leonides Damienides and Rolf Funck. Thanks also go to Paul Geerlings and Myrna Wettke for their dedicated efforts in editing this book. Finally, it goes without saying that all views expressed in the present book are the responsibility of the authors.

Peter Nijkamp
Adriaan Perrels
Amsterdam, September 1993

PART I

SUSTAINABLE CITIES: CHALLENGE AND POTENTIAL OF ENERGY AND ENVIRONMENTAL POLICIES

1

Urban Sustainability as a New Paradigm

SUSTAINABLE CITIES

For many people urban areas are concentration points of environmental decay, where pollution, noise annoyance and congestion can mean a serious threat to human welfare and well-being. At the same time, however, it has to be recognized that – with some ups and downs – urbanization has become widespread around the world, so that at a macro level, apparently, the economies of scale in urban areas are by and large superseding the diseconomies and external costs of modern city life. Nevertheless, the environmental situation in many cities is a matter for concern, as demonstrated by health standards not only in the Third World but also in Europe.

In recent years interest in urban environmental questions has risen to an unprecedented degree. The Commission of the European Communities (EC) launched its Greenbook on the Urban Environment (1990), the Organization for Economic Cooperation and Development (OECD) published its report on Environmental Policies for Cities in the 1990s (1990), while many other institutions (international, national, regional and local) followed this new wave of interest in urban quality of life by organizing meetings of experts, undertaking urban environmental research projects, preparing urban quality of life programmes and the like. Various new concepts were advocated, such as the 'green city', the 'eco-city', the 'liveable city', 'the resourceful city' or the 'environmental city'. Nowadays, apparently, there is a broad concern about the future of our cities (see Elkin et al 1990).

Especially in the European context, the reinforced focus on the city seems warranted, as the European countries (especially those in the EC) are facing a stage of dramatic restructuring and transition as a consequence of the move towards the completion of the internal market. (This follows the Cecchini Report on the economic benefits of the internal market; see Cecchini 1989.) However, the aim to make Europe more competitive in economic terms may be at odds with its environmental sustainability. In the long history of Europe numerous cities with an extremely valuable and vulnerable socio–cultural heritage have emerged which deserve strict protection in the interest of current and future generations. Therefore, what we are facing here is a problem of ecologically sustainable urban development.

The notion of 'sustainable development' has gained much popularity in recent years. The political formulation of this notion is most clearly described in the publication *Our Common Future* (the so-called Brundtland Report; see WCED 1987) as follows: 'a process of change in which the exploitation of resources, the direction of investments, the orientation of technological development and institutional changes are made consistent with future as well as present needs' (p 46). Thus it is clear that the idea of sustainable development is much broader than that of environmental protection. Besides, sustainable development is not a predetermined end state, but a balanced and adaptive evolutionary process. Sustainability refers in this context to a balanced use and management of the natural environmental basis of economic development (see also Archibugi and Nijkamp 1990; Van den Bergh 1991).

Sustainable development has of course a global dimension, but it is also increasingly recognized that there is close mutual interaction between *local* and *global* processes: regions are open systems impacting on all other areas and on the earth as a whole. Therefore, a regional or urban scale for analysing sustainability is certainly warranted. It has to be added that in an open spatial system cross-boundary flows and external development stimuli may play an important role: unsustainability may even be imported or exported. In any case, a focus on local circumstances may enhance our insight into the feasibility of sustainability objectives formulated at a given institutional policy level (Breheny 1992; Giaoutzi and Nijkamp 1993 and Stren 1992).

Sustainability is a concept from (eco-)systems dynamics and refers to the morphogenesis of a dynamic system which is subject to evolutionary change (that is, structural changes in which systems parameters may vary also, in either a linear or a non-linear way). Sustainability in an urban setting, then, describes the potential of a city to reach qualitatively a new level of socio-economic, demographic and technological output which in the long run reinforces the foundations of the urban system, although its evolutionary path may exhibit various stable or unstable temporary fluctuations (Nijkamp 1990). Thus urban sustainability ensures a long-term continuity of the urban system. It is worth noting that we interpret sustainability here at the level of the urban system, and not at the level of the individual players (businesses, households, political parties, and so on). In summary, **sustainable cities are cities where socio–economic interests are brought together in harmony (co-evolution) with environmental and energy concerns in order to ensure continuity in change.**

Thus sustainability is not exactly equal to survival, but means essentially *continuity in changing situations*. These changing situations are clearly reflected in the role of the city, for instance, as an industrial centre, as a service centre, as a high-tech centre, and so on. In the past in most cities it was possible to identify shifts in the role that the city plays within the (changing) national system of cities and within the changing national economy.

Clearly, in some cases war, a catastrophe, the decline of a dominant employer or a major new policy initiative may induce a very clear role change (for example, from an industrial city to a recreational one; from a seaside resort to an electronics centre; from a railway town to a university city, etc). However, in various cases the shifts are not so clear, perhaps, because they have only been partly successful or because countervailing forces emerged to forestall the shift. Interesting examples can be found among large industrial centres which are not regional market and commercial centres (Liverpool, Coventry or Teesside in the UK, for example). In such cities exposure of the export base (both manufacturing and services) of their economies is higher than in the regional 'central place' centres, and hence sustainability would demand a stronger response to the emergence of structural economic upset, disruption and change. The response may be a reassertion of an old role in a new guise (ie with new products and technology), or it may involve role change, through which the whole character of the local economy moves on a fairly rapid transition. Thus sustainability of an urban system will only come into being if the system at hand is exhibiting a high degree of resilience with respect to external and internal challenges.

A situation of *non*-sustainability of a city would imply a structural decline of the economic base of a city (reflected, *inter alia*, in population decline, environmental degradation, inefficient energy systems, loss of employment, emigration of industries and services, and unbalanced social-demographic composition). In general, if the self-organization of an urban system fails (for example, because of lack of consensus among different individual institutions), a phase of non-sustainability is likely to start. Environmental decay is one of the first signs of non-sustainability.

Cities certainly qualify as focal points for sustainability research and planning, as they play a decisive role as nodal points of people and their activities. In many cases they also face the most severe environmental problems, such as air and water pollution, noise, waste, declining quality of urban life and destruction of urban landscapes and architecture – hence the current heightened public awareness and concern about the quality of the urban environment (including public health). Urban policies aiming to achieve sustainable development should be more strategic in nature, more integrative, more visionary regarding the role of the private sector, more focused on the provision of market incentives, and more oriented towards the needs of citizens.

Sustainable urban development has become an important issue in social science research (Banister and Button 1993, Owens 1992 and Rickaby 1991), but the theoretical underpinnings and the critical success parameters of actual urban sustainability policies are still feeble. Moreover, such policies should also cover multiple fields, such as urban rehabilitation and gentrification, land use, transport, energy management, architecture and conservation policy (Newman and Kenworthy 1992). Measurable indicators, including minimum performance levels and critical threshold levels, will then have to be estimated, defined and used in forecasting tools so as to improve awareness of sustainable development issues in modern cities. Local authorities will have to share their tasks with all other players in the urban space (including the private sector). Nevertheless, it goes without saying that urban sustainable development is a process riddled with conflicts and incompatibilities. Key commitment to a strict environmentally sustainable urban development in a city is necessary for a successful implementation of sustainability policies. Economic (market-based) incentives are necessary also in order to cope with the negative externalities of modern city life. Failure to develop an effective balanced urban development policy will reinforce urban sprawl and will spread inner city problems to a much larger area.

The city is – and has always been – the 'home of man' (Ward 1976). Nobody likes to destroy this home, but our current carelessness regarding the daily quality of life threatens to destroy the conditions for the survival and continuity of cities. To counter this, both strong scientific *and* policy interest in the well-being of cities is both warranted and necessary (see also UNEP 1993). Fortunately, there is increasing awareness in Europe and elsewhere that cities need to be sustainable, that is, they should find a development pace which is economically viable without eroding the environmental amenities (both natural and man-made) that make up the foundation stones of social economic progress now and in the future. The question, however, is whether those policies can be identified.

INTEREST IN URBAN QUALITY OF LIFE

Our world is exhibiting a massive transition towards urbanization. The majority of the world population now live in urban areas, and this proportion is still increasing (Juul and Nijkamp 1989). And currently, there are no signs of a change in this pattern of a world-wide urbanization. At face value it seems as though cities are exerting a strong centripetal force, so strong that all negative externalities of the city are to be accepted. However, some words of caution are in order here. Modern cities are suffering severely from environmental overheads (for example Madrid, Rome, Athens, London), and it is precisely these externalities which decide the shape the city will assume in the future. There have been some attempts to design optimal city configurations, eg ideal energy-efficient urban forms (see Owens 1992). Owens proposes spatial models of concentrated deconcentrations as ideal configurations, but the dynamic and structural change in such idealistic models are hard to incorporate.

In order to explain urban dynamics from the viewpoint of urban externalities, it is necessary to recognize that throughout world history, cities have played a critical role as nodal points in the spatial–economic network of a country. This has always attracted urban immigrants in both the developed and the underdeveloped world. However, this movement has at the same time caused urban sprawl, resulting in city regions or functional urban regions. Often both land prices and environmental externalities in central areas of the cities became an impediment for new private and business locations, so that an outward shift began to take place. Industries moved to the urban fringe or to purpose-built industry parks in the city neighbourhoods. People moved to suburban – and even more distant – locations, but essentially this massive movement meant only an expansion of the functional urban territory. Thus, despite a broadening of the spatial range, the urban system has still kept its original function and has even reinforced its position over the past decades. As a consequence, urban environmental damage tends to show a wider spatial coverage (see Orishimo 1982).

Now the question is: how can urban policies be used in order to cope with these urgent issues of urban decay? How can effective instruments be applied so as to improve urban quality of life and to avoid a further spatial

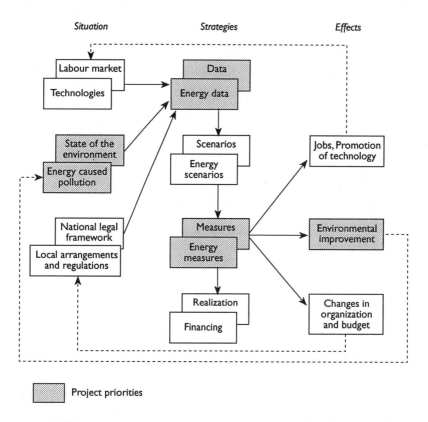

Project priorities

Source: ARP, InnoTec & PEB, Environmental Improvement Model, Report DG XVII, EC, Brussels, 1987

Figure 1.1 Environmental and energy planning in urban systems

distribution of environmental costs? And are such policies of a purely environmental-technological nature only or are they also related to other policy fields, such as transport, housing and physical planning? A good framework for discussing such questions can be found in Figure 1.1, which gives a coherent presentation of environmental and energy planning for a move towards a sustainable city.

A necessary condition for implementing an effective planning system for urban environmental management is the development of a system of suitable urban environmental indicators (see OECD 1978). Such indicators, which should represent a balance between the necessary quality of information and the costs involved, would have to be related to economic, social, spatial and cultural dimensions of the city. The OECD has drawn up a long list of elements which are decisive for urban environmental quality and which would have to be included in such an indicator system. Examples of such indicators are: housing, services and employment, ambient environment and nuisances, social and cultural concerns. However, it appears to be extremely difficult to put such an indicator system for urban sustainability into practice. This means that precise empirical evidence on urban environmental quality and on the implications for both domestic and business behaviour is not always sufficiently available. In the next section, we will first present a few further ideas on urban dynamics, using the above-mentioned notion of urban sustainability as a main frame of reference. We will also discuss briefly residential and entrepreneurial behaviour in a city system, while finally we will turn to urban policy analysis in the field of environmental quality control. We will conclude with some reflective remarks on urban ecology.

URBAN SUSTAINABILITY AS A DEVICE FOR URBAN POLICY

As mentioned in the previous section, the city is the economic, social, cultural and political heart of a society. It provides new impulses and energy for new activities and initiatives. The nodal position of a city in a broader regional, national and international network offers enormous potential with many challenges, but involves at the same time many risks and uncertainties (eg environmental externalities). In the recent past the crucial role of the modern city in a rapidly changing economic and technological environment has fortunately been recognized by many researchers and planners in the urban field (for a broad overview see Nijkamp 1990).

Cities all over the world are experiencing a process of economic restructuring, accompanied by technological transformations and socio-demographic changes. Furthermore, in many countries recent public policies – in the framework of an overall national policy or of regional policies – have shown a marked shift from direct interference to indirect (or conditional) policies (for example incubation policies, innovation policies, and so on). All in all, modern cities tend to show drastic evolutionary changes, in which the human resource potential in a city – comprising creativity, competence and communication (the so-called '3 - C' city) – is playing a dominant role. In this context, technological innovation and new institutional and managerial action lines are increasingly advocated as effective tools in urban and regional development strategies.

The relations between technological change, urban development and environmental conditions deserve much attention. Especially since the widespread urban decline phenomena in the advanced industrial economies from the 1970s, a systematic investigation of these relationships is once more necessary. A major problem in this context, however, is that an integrated and comprehensive theory of the interdependence of urban development, environmental quality and technological innovations is missing.

Currently, most cities exhibit drastic change patterns, varying from rapid decline (in several Western countries) to rapid growth (in new industrialized countries and in boom towns in prosperous areas). Though urban development is a complex and multidimensional phenomenon, it is increasingly realized that – in addition to demographic, social, environmental and residential quality aspects – technology and innovation also may be regarded as major driving forces behind urban economic dynamics. In addition, it is also recognized that a favourable urban structure may stimulate new activities in the city (including new technologies and innovations).

Given the new direction in urban and regional policy with its clear focus on innovations and environmental quality, it is extremely important to pay sufficient attention to the driving forces of urban and regional dynamics. Consequently, much emphasis in urban analyses has to be placed on the selection and assessment of a strategic locational profile in view of long-term changes. Therefore, the geographical aspects of environment and technology call for due attention.

Despite changes in roles and despite stages of relative decline and progress, an indigenous feature of an urban system is its 'struggle for life', in the sense that its final aim will be to continue its existence. However, the aim of continuity is not a random phenomenon, but is to be based on competitive behaviour. Modern cities are indeed operating on a highly competitive (regional and national, but increasingly international) market. Total demand on this broad market is more or less given, and hence the only possibility for an urban system to attract a maximum share of this world market is to be as competitive as possible. In many cases this may require a complete restructuring of the economic, environmental, industrial and technological base of the city. Consequently, continuity or survivorship does by no means imply a stable evolution.

Thus, spatial-economic competition is a basic feature of urban dynamics: the more competitive an urban 'species', the higher its continuity chances. Consequently, this competitive behaviour of cities has to be seen as a rational decision-making process, in which the decision-making agencies are, *inter alia*, the business sector, the public sector, the public at large, and so on. Furthermore, effective and strategic policy measures have to be taken into consideration. The major conventional policy controls of urban management and planning include land use planning, regulation and taxation, investments in infrastructure, operation of public facilities, migration and labour market policies, housing market control and urban taxation schemes. In addition, R&D policy, and communication and information policy may play a crucial role, especially in a long-term perspective.

A common element of urban change processes is inertia (or lack of resilience) in adjustment mechanisms. This may lead to uncoordinated behaviour in housing market, infrastructure, land use, migration and industrialization policies. For instance, the interaction between the production system and a given infrastructure system comprises adjustments which are virtually immediate, given the capacity constraints that prevail at each point in time and space. Changes in capacity constraints and relocations, however, must be filtered through a time consuming decision process. Hence, investment and relocation decisions are delayed in relation to observed noise signals representing under- and over-utilization of existing amenities in the urban system, thus causing unbalanced in- and outflows to and from the city. Urban sprawl is a good example of this.

Urban sprawl rests on a trade-off of agglomeration economies (notably economies of scale and scope including higher wages) versus diseconomies (eg, population density and environmental decay). In most cases the external costs of diseconomies are not (fully) internalized in the price system, so that a distorted urban locational pattern is likely to emerge. In addition, government policies aiming at restoring the balance are often hampered by severe failures, so that the ultimate situation may even get worse. Thus centripetal and centrifugal spatial processes are interchangeably determining the spatial layout of an urban system (city, fringe, rural areas).

Although it is likely that environmental quality problems may become more severe with urban size, there is no clear evidence that urban size as such causes environmental decay. According to Orishimo (1982) and Berry et al (1974) it is not the sheer city size, but rather the land use, the transport system and the spatial layout of a city which are critical factors for urban environmental quality. Thus the attainment of urban sustainability is undoubtedly a complex and dynamic problem.

ECONOMIC ACTIVITIES AND THE URBAN SYSTEM

Urban (or metropolitan) regions are essentially large production and information processing systems encompassing the core economic activities of a country and acting as the focal point of an inter-urban, regional or national network. Clearly, the structure of such regions may exhibit a great diversity ranging from large scale industrial complexes (for example the greater Rotterdam area) to large business service centres (for example the greater Amsterdam area). The evolutionary path of such areas does not only reflect stages of fast growth and stagnant maturity, but also obsolescence and decline. Over time, these areas may show drastic changes in the degree of specialization in the economic system (for example the *Twente* area in the Netherlands moved gradually from a traditional textile-oriented structure into an information-oriented structure). Inertia, resilience and revival appear to be characteristic features of modern urban areas.

Like all competitive dynamic systems, urban systems may be regarded as biological species, evolving with different growth rates and in different directions. Clearly this process has strong spatial implications. Migration and relocation processes of firms and households, however, are not merely reactions to economic developments, but also have their own dynamics such as product life cycles and demographic cycles. Consequently, despite much variety there are also evolutionary patterns which are common to all urban systems.

It is not only economic activities that show an evolutionary trend, but also all related physical elements (eg infrastructure). When more and more space in central locations becomes occupied by buildings, facilities and other physical, durable structures, the activity density (and intensity) increases. The inertia embodied in a fixed structure affects the competitive power of the areas at hand, so that a process of decline may start. The city of Amsterdam is a good example of this phenomenon, since its historical character precludes a flexible adjustment to structural changes. This explains why most new (high tech and business services oriented) firms locate in more spacious and accessible areas around Amsterdam. Thus conventional city centres tend to lose part of their innovation and incubation potential in favour of their outskirts (see Davelaar and Nijkamp 1989).

In the framework of metropolitan dynamics, there also appears to be a link between the stages of metropolitan development (defined in terms of population or jobs) and economic development. The early urban concentration phase can usually be observed together with an early industrialization phase, where people and jobs concentrate in the already existing urban areas, characterized by the best infrastructure available at the time. As industrialization proceeds and per capita incomes rise, the demand for new housing as well as for gardens and parks, etc leads to suburbanization. As the network of public and private infrastructure increasingly covers the whole country, urban areas appear to lose their comparative economic advantages and jobs begin to decentralize. In the post-industrial society, de-urbanization seems to have become a widespread phenomenon. It should be added however, that this de-urbanization movement generally affects relatively small-scale urbanized centres which are functionally dependent on the main centres. Thus to some extent the de-urbanization phenomenon is a natural consequence of earlier urbanization rather than a new development. In the context of this hypothesis, the de-urbanization phase should be followed by re-urbanization. Although this trend cannot yet be firmly established statistically, there are some signals which indicate that urban renewal in old city centres does, in fact, lead to increases in economic activity (gentrification).

In light of the above mentioned evolutionary patterns of cities, it is desirable to draw on principles of dynamic systems in order to gain a full understanding of the forces at work. In this context, some notions from population dynamics and ecology may be useful. Essentially, cities may be regarded as competing species which strive for continuity (sometimes even survival) and territorial expansion. Cohabitation (on the basis of complementarity) or extinction (on the basis of competition) are two extreme possibilities of the evolutionary process of species. Thus we need to take a closer look at the 'objectives' of each species in order to understand its dynamics.

One may argue that sustainability – as a social science interpretation of the continuity objective of a species – may be conceived as a plausible development objective of a city in competition with other cities. Sustainability may be regarded as the (implicit) ultimate goal of a dynamic multi-actor system in which each actor is trying to achieve his own goals. An extreme emphasis on pursuing one's own goal may render one's own strategies futile due to 'countervailing power' of other actors. Thus, despite fluctuations and structural changes, a dynamic multi-actor system tends to move along a certain stable path in order to guarantee its own long-term continuity. The notion of sustainability is thus essentially broader than that of stability. Stability neglects the morpho–genetic properties of a dynamic system, so that fluctuating patterns which might in the long run be necessary for survival are excluded. Thus sustainability leaves open the possibility of self-adjustment of a system even if this may temporarily imply wild fluctuations, an observation which is also made in recent spatial applications of chaos theory (Nijkamp and Reggiani 1992).

URBAN SUSTAINABILITY AND ECOLOGY

Modern urban systems – with their high density of population and economic activities, their nodal position in interwoven geographical and functional–economic (inter)national networks and their ambition to act as engines in the competitive process of open regions – are faced with increasing environmental problems. These range from air, soil and water pollution to intangible externalities such as noise annoyance, lack of safety, destruction of 'cityscape', or visual pollution. Clearly, there is a wide variety of sources generating these urban environmental problems, including demographic factors, socio–economic development, inefficient energy consumption, inappropriate technologies, spatial behavioural patterns, and most important of all, inappropriate and/or badly enforced urban environmental policy measures (see Rickaby 1991). Thus an improvement of the current unfavourable situation requires a mobilization of all forces.

Recently a new discipline has arisen, called **urban ecology**. This aims to design principles for sound urban environmental policy (see also Marahrens et al, 1991), examples of which are:

- minimize space consumption in urban areas (eg underground parking areas);
- minimize spatial mobility in the urban space by reducing the geographical separation between working, living and facility spaces;
- minimize urban private transport;
- favour the use of new information technology and telecommunication technology;
- minimize urban waste and favour recycling;
- minimize urban energy use (eg combined heat and power systems, district heating etc).

Several of these ideas will also be considered in our framework for sustainable cities in Europe.

Such principles are somewhat comparable to those formulated in the so called **Gaia concept** (see Lovelock 1979). The fulfilment of such principles will of course require an effective urban policy, which is multi-faceted in nature and covers a great many aspects of current city life. Once implemented, they might turn cities into 'islands of renewal in seas of decay' (Berry 1985). Cities and regions would then have to play a much more active role by mobilizing all actors in the urban territory and by playing a missionary role in convincing them that a sustainable city means a sustainable economy and society. An interesting illustration of concrete attempts at achieving sustainable cities can be found in the Danish 'Green Municipality Project' in which various cities in Denmark collaborate with the aim to generate awareness and policy actions at the local level in order to pave the way for economically and ecologically responsible development of cities. Various pilot projects (called *green projects*) have been initiated which focus attention on lifestyles, health care, education/information, landscape, clean technology, water management, energy policy, transport and built environment in the city. In Germany a similar project between cooperating cities has recently started, called 'OEKO CEPT', which aims to introduce and operationalize ecologically-based concepts and paradigms in urban planning and urban renewal.

Besides national initiatives we observe increasingly also international (mainly European) plans where cities wish to cooperate in the areas of urban environmental and energy policy, the main objective being to exchange information on experiences, successful or otherwise, regarding urban environmental policy measures. One of such initiatives is the CITIES programme (Community Integrated Task for the Improvement of Energy-Environmental Systems in Cities), launched by the Commission of the European Communities (EC). In Part B of this book various results and experiences from the CITIES programme will be presented.

However, recent experiences have made clear that the route towards sustainable urban development is paved with many stumbling blocks.

A few caveats in achieving an operational policy for sustainable cities will be mentioned here.

- The **profile** of a 'sustainable city ' is not unambiguous and always appears to generate a lot of debate (eg a focus on a tourist city, a cultural city, a service city etc).
- The **policy sectors** to be considered in a sustainable city policy may show much variation (eg industry, transport, public services, recreation, energy).
- The definition and measurement of various (socio–economic, spatial and environmental) **policy indicators** are fraught with many uncertainties.
- The steps from measurement of indicators via identification of bottlenecks to exploration and implementation of successful **sustainability policy measures** have seldom been undertaken.
- Changes in **urban land use** involving a **substitution** between different activities (eg a parking place into office space) provoke much discussion on the tradeoffs between the socio–economic and environmental implications and evaluation of such changes.
- **Financial budgets** of cities impose severe constraints on the flexibility and feasibility of new urban environmental plans.
- **Small-scale improvements in the direct living environment** of urban inhabitants are often much higher valued than strategic urban development plans.
- **Transport in the city** appears to lead to many externalities which are however extremely hard to cope with.
- **Integrated urban environmental policy** (the so-called 'chain' concept, from a source to an end) has not yet become a widely accepted idea.

In light of the previous observations, the conclusion seems warranted that the road towards sustainable cities is not an easy one. High ambitions seem to meet fierce resistance and therefore some moderation seems to be necessary. Nevertheless, various successes in European cities can be observed which certainly deserve more attention. Especially in the field of integrated urban energy planning – which is to a large extent forming the basis for urban environmental planning – various noticeable experiences can be found. The next chapter will provide a more comprehensive survey of the potential of combined urban energy–environmental policy as a vehicle for a sustainable city.

2

Energy–Environmental Policy as a Focal Point of Sustainable Cities

ENERGY–ENVIRONMENTAL POLICY: MACRO OBJECTIVES, LOCAL IMPLEMENTATION

Since the first oil crisis in 1973, energy policy has gained importance in the industrialized world. Energy savings measures have been implemented in many industrial sectors, in the household sector and also – with varying degrees of success – in different cities all over the world. In the past fifteen years, energy efficiency (in terms of the ratio between gross national product and energy consumption) has increased by approximately 20 to 25 per cent. And recent estimates suggest that another increase of the order of magnitude of 30 per cent over the next ten to fifteen years is certainly possible. The following factors may explain this trend towards a further rise in energy productivity:

Economic factors

The economies in the western world have become much more competitive – and thus more cost-sensitive – and hence any reduction in costs (either in the energy sector or elsewhere) is always welcome to businesses; it is foreseeable that the trend towards an open European Market with more competition will stimulate a further energy cost awareness, as cost-effectiveness of urban energy–environmental policy is of paramount importance.

Structural shifts

There is an increasing trend for an industrialized society to develop towards a service-oriented society; this so-called de-industrialization process has led to less energy-intensive production methods, and it is plausible to assume that the share of energy in national production in many countries will further decline (even irrespective of energy savings measures).

Policy programmes

In many countries intensified efforts have been made in the past decade to induce more energy-efficient modes of production, transport and consumption. A variety of policy measures has been devised in this context, for example, grants and loans for new energy technologies, taxes and charges on existing less efficient energy use, and new institutional arrangements and regulations.

In light of the previous observations the question may be raised whether there is still a need for an intensification of energy planning. It seems almost paradoxical to place even more emphasis on energy savings measures, if energy prices are relatively low. However, there are various convincing reasons which justify a large scale effort at improving the current energy situation in Europe:

- The principle of **economic efficiency**, which teaches us that in a competitive international economy cost-saving measures in all respects are a *sine qua non*.
- The need for **appropriate resource management**, which suggests that, in view of risk strategies and energy scarcities, continuous efforts are to be made to ensure resource availability in the long run.
- The political goal of favouring **ecologically sustainable economic development** (in the spirit of the Brundtland Report), so that a joint endeavour has to be made to incorporate environmental considerations in energy management (see also Chapter 1).

In the past ten years, energy management has exhibited some dramatic shifts associated with the changes in the general political climate in Europe. We see the following broad trends emerging:

- **Deregulation:** the removal of unnecessary administrative, institutional or bureaucratic barriers.
- **Decentralisation:** a devolution of the responsibility for energy policy (and production) from centralized energy agencies towards decentralized agencies at local and regional levels.
- **Diversification:** a transition from a single resource orientation (eg oil) towards a multiple resource orientation.
- **Market orientation:** a tendency to be more competitive on the basis of market signals and prices.

In the meantime governments, energy producers, industries and consumers have implemented – often with considerable success – a great diversity of energy conservation plans. This has led to significant reductions in energy needed to heat dwellings, drive cars or produce agricultural or industrial products. In a recent report of the IEA (1987), it was assessed that the amount of energy used to produce one unit of gross domestic product (being an indicator for energy intensity) fell by approximately 20 per cent between 1973 and 1985. Especially in the industrial sector the energy efficiency increased considerably, while also the residential/commercial sector achieved a much higher efficiency of energy use than in the past. However, the efficiency of electricity generation did not rise very much. Moreover, a part of the increase in energy efficiency should not be attributed to energy savings policies but to structural changes in the economy, which generally meant a shift from basic to non-basic industries and services. This observation exemplifies the savings potential yet to be tapped.

A significant part of the success of energy conservation policies can be attributed to various financial incentives programmes. Examples in various sectors are:

- *Industry*:

  - grants to stimulate energy conservation investments
  - tax incentives to encourage energy efficient production processes
  - loans to stimulate less energy-intensive capital investments.

- *Residential/commercial sector*:

  - grants to help develop energy conservation schemes
  - tax incentives to induce building insulation
  - loans for specific energy conservation purposes.

In addition, in various countries information programmes (eg publicity campaigns, residential and industrial energy audits, appliance labelling or transportation fuel efficiency information) and regulation/standard systems (for example building codes, appliance efficiency standards, fuel economy standards for new passenger cars) have been introduced as a policy tool to increase energy awareness.

Despite the improvement of energy efficiency in the past fifteen years, there is still much scope for further energy improvements in all end-use sectors. According to the above mentioned report, it is quite feasible that, if energy conservation measures which are now economically viable were fully implemented by the year 2000, energy intensity would even fall down to 30 per cent below the current levels.

As a result we have observed the need for, and the emergence of, more focused and customized energy programmes, and it is no surprise that in this context local and regional energy planning has become a major focal point. Nowadays local energy initiatives seem to offer a wide spectrum of new possibilities for enhancing energy efficiency and hence improving local environmental quality (see also MacKerron 1989). Such local initiatives have many advantages, such as:

- **effectiveness of energy strategies**: they are usually based on feasible and concrete measures at a local scale (eg district heating);
- **cost efficiency**: they try to devise new energy use patterns which are beneficial for the community at large;
- **flexibility**: they are not based on rigid national views, but on tailor-made local policy action;

- **marketing and implementation**: they are much more able to obtain local support, as they are able to communicate new energy options directly to the local population;
- **environmental quality**: they can directly benefit from the environmental consciousness at local or regional levels.

The main focus of this book is on urban energy policy and its spinoffs for urban environmental management. Although energy policy has its own indigenous merits and although urban sustainability is much broader than energy policy, it is at the same time clear that urban energy policy is an extremely important point of departure for urban sustainability policy.

Energy and environmental issues are increasingly regarded as two sides of the same coin. The initial concern about the global energy situation during the seventies (the first energy crisis) was based mainly on the threats of a depletion of energy resources. Consequently this situation led to many efforts in most countries to reduce their vulnerability with respect to excessively fluctuating energy prices. Nowadays, although the latter phenomenon is still a significant factor (usually in conjunction with security of supply), in most national energy policy schemes environmental factors appear to receive increasing attention.

Energy policy objectives may – at least partly – be achieved by means of national measures, notably the manipulation of prices (including taxes and subsidies). For instance, the improvement of energy efficiency will certainly be stimulated by high energy prices. Also the introduction of new major energy sources, such as nuclear energy, is usually a national policy item. However, both the residential sector and small and medium sized firms need more stimuli than just price incentives to ensure that they are actually participating in energy efficiency activities. Demonstration, information, consultancy and individual client-oriented treatment are, in many countries, the usual non-price ingredients of energy policy schemes in a decentralized setting. To ensure sufficient impact these national instruments should be easily accessible for the target groups concerned. In practice this means that their implementation should be realized at a regional or local level.

Environmental policy focusing on sustainable development has – compared to energy policy – to rely even more on non-price instruments, such as national, or preferably international, standards. Regarding the motivation of target groups, environmental policy has to take into consideration the local environmental, social and economic situation. Therefore decentralization of the implementation of environmental policy schemes is at least as strong a prerequisite as it is for energy policy schemes.

In recent years the interest in local and regional environmental and energy policies has shown a remarkable rise. After the era of nationwide and/or sectoral energy–environmental policies, it has been realized that cities and regions form important focal points for integrative and effective energy saving and environmental protection strategies with a view on both economizing on resource expenditures and improving environmental quality. Often cities and regions are fairly coherent administrative units, have a joint energy production unit, a direct interest in resource and environment issues and – usually – an abundance of statistical material. As a consequence, urban and regional energy and environmental planning is gaining increasing importance as an effective strategy for ensuring ecologically sustainable economic development, as advocated in the Brundtland report (see also Juul and Nijkamp 1988, and Nijkamp and Volwahsen 1990). Cities are able to offer, in principle, a wide variety of energy and environmental strategies. In addition to the national level, regional and local energy measures often turn out to be indispensable additions to national policies. Moreover, some problems are typically local in nature and may preferably be dealt with at the local level.

The institutional setting in which the energy and environmental system operates is of paramount importance to the feasibility and effectiveness of any local energy policy. Therefore, special attention should be given to institutional aspects.

The structure of energy production, supply and distribution exhibits – in terms of ownership, organization and regulation – a remarkable variety among European countries. For instance, ownership structures range from entirely publicly owned energy systems to those where privately owned utilities dominate (see Helm and McGowan 1987). Similarly, depending on the specific fuel source and political structures in a given country, one finds organizational configurations ranging from nationalization/ centralization to privatization/decentralization. Centralized energy systems used to exist in the UK and France, while decentralized systems used to be present in the Netherlands (with a strong influence of communal authorities) and Germany (with a strong influence of regional authorities). Mixed structures can be found *inter alia* in Sweden. In recent years there is a tendency, in several European countries, to separate electricity production from distribution, in order to gain economies of scale in production as well as to reorganize distribution at the regional or local level. This separation aims at increasing competition in production and a customer orientation among distribution companies.

In view of the trend toward a stronger market orientation and more deregulation/privatization (seeking to use the market mechanism as a competitive tool for increasing efficiency), there is, in most countries, an increasing tendency toward more flexibility regarding energy supply and distribution at a local level. Private–public oriented district heating systems, privately based industrial co-generation systems and private solar and wind energy systems are increasingly emerging. Consequently, public–private partnership as new organizational forms for local energy provision and distribution are becoming increasingly popular. Thus it seems reasonable to assume that, at the local (urban or communal) level where the institutional structures are in general less complex and less multi-faceted than at country/provincial levels, there is much scope for well focused and tailor made energy programmes at a decentralized level. Since most people live in cities and since most economic activities take place in urban areas, it goes without saying that urban energy conservation plans are an important component of energy–environmental policy aimed at a further improvement of energy efficiency and local environmental quality.

This observation makes even more sense if we realize that according to recent estimates (IEA 1986), 34 per cent of total final energy consumption is caused by the maintenance and use of commercial, public and residental buildings, most of them being located in urban areas. Both Individual Dedicated Control (IDC) technologies (for example heat production, air conditioning control) and Comprehensive Energy Management and Control Systems (CEMCS) technologies (for example load management, remote energy monitoring and control district heating) may be used here as effective vehicles for further energy savings.

There is another reason why decentralized energy systems seem to gain popularity, namely the interrelationship between energy and environmental conditions. The generation, conversion and use of energy has usually very detrimental effects on the environment (for example due to emission of SO_2, NO_x, CO, PCB and particles). The environmental awareness at local levels has led to much resistance against expansion programmes of energy power plants in the vicinity of urban areas. And there is an increasing trend towards setting strict emission standards for combustion plants, cars and so on (eg limitations on sulphur content in fuel oils and lead content in gasoline). In this respect, efficient local energy planning and effective local environmental management have similar interests. This also explains the broad support for district heating systems and combined heat/power systems at the level of urban agglomerations. Especially at a decentralized level a reconciliation and coordination of energy and environmental policies is likely to become an effective and appropriate policy strategy. This observation is also supported by information from a broad international overview of energy policies and programmes in various countries (IEA 1988).

MOTIVES FOR AN URBAN ORIENTATION

In the past decade, the efficient use of energy did not seem to be an acute issue from the point of view of availability of energy resources. The Gulf crisis has proven that this was a typically short-sighted viewpoint. The geographical and often political imbalance between spatial concentrations of oil supply and demand may be expected to be a continuous source of global oil market disturbances; hence reliable alternative sources – including savings – remain a sound strategic energy policy option.

Besides this consideration of energy availability we have to add the important environmental concerns. Moreover, as long as fossil fuels dominate the energy mix, the exhaustibility of these resources should not be overlooked, particularly in view of significantly rising extraction costs. Finally, in a competitive European economy cost efficient production is of utmost importance, so that energy consumption will remain a major concern in the economic activities of firms in the next decades.

Urban areas are by definition centres of economic activity. Given that a concentration of activities implies a concentration of energy supply, urban areas, (next to the international, national and regional level), seem to be a suitable geographical entity as a focus for energy policy. Admittedly, large energy consuming industries have usually relocated themselves from the core areas to the urban fringe, but that leaves the notion of urban areas as large concentrations of (direct and indirect) energy users, both for production and consumption, essentially unaffected. It is certainly true that the majority of Europeans live in urban areas, and that makes these areas suitable as focal points of energy-environmental policies.

Despite major global issues, like the global warming effect, it is still important to realize that most of these background factors are – directly or indirectly – related to urban activities. Thus cities play an important role in a sustainable development policy and they have to be considered as centres for sustainability policies. This of course is true also for cities in Eastern Europe and in Third World countries, but in principle this mission applies to all cities.

Furthermore, the decentralization argument in environmental–energy policy also has an important function in a bottom-up policy strategy, as it will usually require less efforts to involve and to motivate local inhabitants and interest groups for energy conservation and environmental programmes.

In light of the above observations, one may thus distinguish the following reasons why a well focused energy-environmental planning strategy at the urban level is a potentially valuable activity in the framework of sustainable urban development.

First, there is the obvious reason that most production, consumption and transportation activities in a country take place in urban areas. It is noteworthy that in most countries the level of urbanization is still increasing, not only in prosperous regions but also in less favoured regions. Thus a clear focus on urban energy planning may enhance the effectiveness of energy and environmental strategies in many countries.

Next, decentralization of energy and related environmental policy has become a major device in current policy-making in most Western countries. The city is of course a natural institutional decision unit in this context, as it covers a well focused study area without running the risk of a heterogeneous policy stucture with many horizontally organized planning agencies (and related competence questions). Thus the involvement of one identifiable decision-making agency at the urban level is of a major importance and may enhance the institutional effectiveness of energy and environmental planning.

A related obvious advantage may be the direct local involvement, based on a bottom-up strategy for new energy saving programmes and related environmental management programmes (for instance, in the case of district heating). This may increase the support of the general public for changes in energy production and/or consumption patterns.

Finally, in terms of efficiency of data gathering and/or availability, the city is usually a more suitable statistical entity providing systematic data sets on environmental, energy and socio–economic indicators.

Thus the foreseeable advantages of regional energy planning at the urban level are:

1.   more effective actions from municipal energy agencies and
2.   a closer involvement of urban residents/entrepreneurs in the triangle of energy, environmental and economy.

There are various ways of saving energy in the urban environment. Household activities and consumption, industrial and commercial activities, and transportation are – in addition to electricity production – the main sources of energy use. Many European experiences have shown that considerable savings are still possible.

In industry new technologies and better insulation of buildings may lead to a considerable rise of energy efficiency, although this clearly has a long lead time in normal circumstances. In the residential sector, housing insulation programmes may also lead to drastic energy savings for both space heating and air conditioning (eg by means of better insulation, heat pumps, solar energy installations, wind turbines, and economisers for central heating systems). Also in the transport sector considerable savings are, in principle, possible (for example through more energy-efficient engines, vehicle weight reduction or – in the long run – through more energy-efficient physical planning aimed at a reduction of commuting distance and/or a shift of the modal split in favour of public transport).

At a more integrated and intermediate level of urban energy planning, various possibilities are offered by central heat distribution, by recycling of energy from heat, by combined heat and power either in district heating or in cogeneration, or by using urban/industrial waste as a fuel for generating plants. Especially at a local level these energy saving options are likely to be more efficient than at a more regional level, as generally such options require fairly high densities of energy demand (see Hutchinson 1991).

An example of the possible gains of energy efficiency to be achieved if various cities intensify their efforts at establishing systems of district heating can be found in Figure 2.1.

In general, urban energy planning may comprise a whole set of different and complementary energy policy strategies ('packaging' of policy measures), such as industrial cogeneration, district heating, combined heat and power (CHP) generation (using steam turbines, internal combustion engines, gas turbines or combined cycle gas turbines), combined urban waste management and energy production, load management, and institutional reforms in the structure of utilities. Various European cities provide good examples of the potential of urban energy planning: Berlin, Amsterdam, Gothenburg, Torino, Rennes and Grenoble.

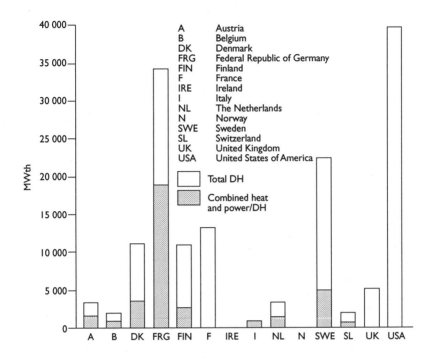

Source: Rüdig (1986)

Figure 2.1 Potential penetration of district heating (DH) in various countries

In recent years the insight has grown that urban energy planning may generate many economic and environmental advantages. So far, however, there has been no systematic evaluation of urban energy programmes or experiences in different European countries. The experiences so far gathered from regional energy planning studies sponsored by the Commission of European Communities are important here, even though manifest differences (for example in terms of institutional competence and forms) do exist. There is certainly a need for more constructive and strategic reflections on the feasibility of urban energy planning.

In conclusion, it is a favourable circumstance that urban energy planning seems to be a new departure in energy management in Europe (see Juul and Nijkamp 1989). There is increasing interest in systematic European efficient and effective energy policies through the medium of decentralized, local initiatives.

3

Recent Developments in Local Energy and Environmental Planning

INTRODUCTION

The previous chapters have outlined the framework for sustainable cities. Such cities aim at achieving a balanced (*co-evolutionary*) development in which economic forces (for example efficiency), social considerations (for example equity and access to facilities) and environmental concerns (for example quality of life) are brought together from the viewpoint of a 'green society' (see also Pearce et al 1989). Enhancing local energy efficiency is likely to be one of the critical success factors for sustainable cities, as wise energy management and use provides a substantial support to an improvement of the local economy, such as a higher degree of competitiveness, to a more affordable – and hence equitable – distribution of scarce resources (ie a better access to public services) and to a reduction in the environmental burden (for example a reduction in emissions of CO_2). Thus a more sustainable form of urban development requires an increase in demand to reduce the consumption of fossil fuels, for instance, through the introduction of district heating, cogeneration or combined heat and power (CHP) technologies.

The main problem in building 'sustainable cities' is *not* the lack of arguments supporting the need for 'green based' cities, but the question of designing proper concrete co-evolutionary urban development strategies that can boast sufficient public support. As our societies – and our cities – move more towards the end of the 20th century, the case for improving drastically the energy and environmental base of our cities takes on a steadily growing importance and urgency. If modern cities want to maintain and improve their role as the 'home of man' (Ward 1976), intensified efforts are needed to safeguard both the historical-cultural heritage left to the present generation by its predecessors and the socioeconomic and environmental potential of modern cities needed to host the future generation. Local energy and environmental planning is then a *sine qua non* for the fulfilment of the latter task. In the present chapter we will describe some trends in local/regional environmental and energy analysis.

THE CHANGING CONTEXT OF ENERGY AND ENVIRONMENTAL PLANNING

Some trends

Since the 1970s, energy and environmental issues have played an important role in all countries. They have also provoked many conflicts. It is likely that these issues will remain one of the focal points of policy interest, not only at the national level, but also at the urban/regional level. Energy has become a strategic production factor that contributes significantly to the prosperity of regions and nations. At the same time energy generation and use (for example in transport, industry, households) has caused severe environmental damage in all countries and cities.

Policymakers in various countries and cities have recognized the importance of a well-balanced and coherent energy strategy in order to safeguard the conditions for uninterrupted economic development, but have at the same time stressed the need for effective and efficient energy management at a decentralized level. In this context, local and regional energy planning has demonstrated its validity as an operational and strategic policy effort for an economical use of scarce energy resources in a given administrative area.

At the same time, it is also realized increasingly that energy production and/or consumption may have dramatic environmental impacts on a local or regional scale. There is no country or region which is not suffering from environmental decay caused by the energy sector. Besides, it is also evident that there is a close connection between local (ie regional and urban) development on the one hand and environmental conditions on the other. It is therefore necessary to incorporate regional and urban development and environmental quality aspects in regional and urban energy analyses (see Hafkamp 1986). These observations can briefly be represented by means of the following scheme:

Energy		Urban activities		Urban environmental
Other inputs	$\longrightarrow$	Land use	$\longrightarrow$	quality

Generally speaking, the following three developments seem to influence energy planning in many countries today:

1. The transition from cheap and abundant oil supplies towards a broader mix of energy carriers and new conservation technologies appear to offer a strong economic stimulus for some regions but, conversely, it also involves an additional threat of economic decay to other regions. A strict oil dependence makes both the supplier and demander vulnerable.
2. Thoughtless energy use is the primary cause of an accelerating deterioration of the natural environment all over Europe. Any attempt by public authorities to improve regional and urban environmental

conditions requires a better knowledge about the respective chains of causes, time delays and effects.

3. Environmental protection policy is – at least in the short term – accompanied by a series of vital conflicts with local or regional polluting industries and activities (for example transport). Any imposition of reasonable restrictions on economic activities (including energy production, conversion and use) also influences the competitive position of the respective regions and may generate in the short run fierce resistance.

Given these conditions, it is appropriate to investigate in more detail the triangular relationship and possible synergisms between energy systems, regional development and environmental management from a sustainability viewpoint. For the sake of brevity we will use here the generic term 'regional development' for local, urban or regional development. Now the three sides of this triangle will be discussed.

Energy systems and environmental quality

Energy conversion and use are nowadays major sources of environmental pollution in most industrialized regions: burning liquid fuels in transportation accounts for most of the emissions of nitrogen oxides; the combustion of hydrocarbons in thermal power plants accounts for most of the sulphur dioxides, carbon dioxide, trace metals, etc. In addition, water and waste pollution, extensive use of land, soil contamination and so on are aggravated by energy use. Increasing pollution levels call for technical, organizational and institutional actions in many countries.

In this context, three strategies may be envisaged:

*   **Strategy 1:** Reduce emissions by means of *abatement* techniques, for instance by adding filters and other new equipment to conversion processes.
*   **Strategy 2:** Reduce emissions (and risks) by means of *substitution* techniques, such as a switch from polluting energy carriers to less polluting energies such as renewable resources.
*   **Strategy 3:** Reduce emissions by means of *preventive* techniques, by for example reducing energy demand, because the comparatively high level of energy consumption in industrialized parts of the world is not sustainable in the long run, from neither economic or environmental aspects.

Strategy 1 means shifting part of the pollution into other environmental media. For instance, flue-gas cleaning produces substantial amounts of waste pollution; catalytic processes to reduce nitrogen oxides add to water pollution, and so on.

Strategy 2 relocates, to a certain extent, environmental loads and risks (planting bioalcohol, for instance, leads to long-range soil deterioration; windmills or solar energy consume land and affect the visual beauty of landscapes, and so on).

Strategy 3 represents the ecologically most feasible strategy, as it is designed to reduce generally the cycle of substances by savings techniques and recycling.

All three strategies demand substantial capital investment. Strategy 1 also increases operating costs; strategy 2 calls for incentives for investments to start substitution processes; and strategy 3 implies a substitution of operating costs by capital costs, as costs for energy consumption are saved. In a macro-economic sense, capital costs are often favoured by politicians, as this may mean technological progress and job creation. Technological strategies for strategy 3 are, *inter alia*, energy management systems, reduction in energy needs, heat recovery, heat pumps, exploiting endogenous sources such as waste, and so on. Quite often these investments have short payback periods; they may very well be the starting point for an overall modernization of enterprises. They may also require significant changes in public energy companies, as will be discussed later on.

Environmental quality and regional development

Regional development is not necessarily at odds with a favourable environmental quality, and certainly not in the long run. A high environmental quality offers a great potential for many activities such as recreation, tourism and research, without significant negative externalities. However, an overuse of scarce environmental resources will not only deteriorate environmental conditions, but is in the long run also detrimental to the local or regional economy. A good quality of life is often an important locational motive for new entrepreneurs. Thus it is in the interest of the economy at large when the highest possible environmental quality is strived for (see also Nijkamp and Soeteman 1990).

Densely populated regions such as Athens or Mexico, or industrial regions (like the Rhein–Ruhr area) with high energy consumption levels show a proportionally low level of environmental quality. In most countries the worsening environmental situation has usually been coped with by legal actions, such as regulating lower emission levels, thus imposing barriers for further economic development. An example of this strategy in the 1980s can be found in the Dutch Selective Investment Regulation (SIR), which incorporated a system of taxes on new industrial investments, when these investments were implemented in environmentally vulnerable or densely populated areas, in particular the Dutch conurbation of the Randstad (although during the recession period this law was abolished).

Favourable environmental quality, on the other hand, is an explicit locational criterion for quite a few advanced technologies. For instance, the least polluted regions in Europe like southern France, Baden-Württemberg and Scotland turn out to be particularly attractive for high tech firms. Thus environmental quality also offers potential for a region's development. In conclusion, the relationship between regional development and environmental quality can be either supportive or mutually conflicting.

Regional development and energy systems

A series of impact studies undertaken in all parts of the world point to the important role of energy systems in the development of a regional economy. At the *intraregional* level, a rationalization of energy conversion and energy use may lead to the application of advanced technologies. An increased efficiency may reduce primary energy input; a high level of managerial skill may reduce the consumption of resources; improved control and supervision techniques may decrease the demand for human labour. Thus overall costs may then be reduced, while environmental performance may be improved. The modernization of enterprises will in this sense enhance the competitiveness of regions in the future; a higher level of environmental quality will allow for the location of new enterprises, and this again may improve local labour market, as higher qualifications are needed. Thus the achievement of high environmental quality may also enhance the regional development potential in the medium and long term.

At the *interregional* level, it should be noted that a regional system is an open and connected system, so that policy measures in one area have an influence on other areas. For instance, a switch from oil to wind energy in Denmark has an impact on acid rain in Scandinavia. Energy policy decisions at a national or EC level influence regional economies in several respects. Some illustrative examples are:

- Regional labour market changes may result from changes in the mix of primary energies produced (for example, the number of jobs in the coal mining industry in Belgium, the UK and Germany has dropped sharply since 1950) and from the relocation of conversion plants (the refinery capacity in many European regions has dropped since oil-producing countries increased their own refinery capacity).
- Energy-dependent (or energy-related) industries tend to concentrate geographically near energy conversion sites. Aluminium production plants, for example, have to locate closely to base-load power plants. Regions with a high potential for wind energy succeed in building up an internationally successful wind turbine industry (Denmark), while regions with mineral oil production experience a boom in the construction industry and hence face a considerable reduction in regional unemployment (Shetland Islands).

The triangle revisited

The examples given above are certainly not an exhaustive description of cross-impacts between energy systems, regional development and environmental quality. They may, however, help to define in a given region a more systematic and comprehensive list of impacts to be observed. It should be added that the three corner points of the region–energy–environment triangle are not necessarily barriers to each other, but may also be mutually supportive. Regional energy planning should strive to exploit the potential offered by these three angles. This requires the assessment of a broad range of impacts.

For large-scale energy projects, such an attempt has occasionally been undertaken. Table 3.1 shows a typical checklist for such evaluations. At a regional scale, which is sometimes also focusing on small- or medium-sized projects, the impacts listed in Table 3.1 are perhaps not always measurable, especially as far as the Social system/Institutions subsystem is concerned, but nevertheless this scheme portrays a series of relevant impacts, which might be used as a checklist during the initial planning stage.

Table 3.1. The various impacts of large-scale energy projects.

Source: Johansson and Lakshmanan (1985)

Sector	Types of impacts
Energy	
Demand:	Level and composition; shifts between types (forms) of energy and between local/regional and external supply sources; changes in energy-use technologies.
Supply of primary energy:	Identification and utilization of resources and reserves.
Supply technologies:	Composition of the system of energy conversion chains. Technical change.
Other systemic effects:	Complementarity and substitution between components of the supply system.
Economy	
Production/supply and demand:	Development of sectors such as industry, transportation and communication, residential, services.
Capital formation:	Construction and installation of fixed capital; financing investments.
Employment:	Supply and demand for labour; employment and participation rates.
'Market' effects:	Prices, wages, shortages, queues, etc; export/import balances; fiscal effects.
Household/welfare:	Income and wealth, employment opportunities; distribution between individuals and socioeconomic groups.
Social system/institutions	
Migration and population change:	Number and categories of migrating households; turnover rate for categories of households, etc.
Community growth:	New settlements, new infrastructure, and public capital.
Social tensions:	Household stability, criminal activity, etc.
Tensions in the public sector:	Public sector budgeting, financing investments in schools, health care, etc.
Institutional spatial conflicts:	Distribution of costs and benefits between municipalities; interregional, interstate and intercountry impacts like acid rain, etc.
Land-use patterns	
Induced governmental decisions	
Environment	
Atmosphere:	Air quality; pollutants, visibility etc.
Water system:	Water quality: pollutants, temperature, etc
Land-use patterns:	Changing areas for production, recreation, wildlife, etc.
Ecological systems	
Solid and hazardous wastes	
Climatic changes	

In general, there appears to be a clear need for an integrated approach to energy–environmental problems at the local level (see Van den Bergh 1991). This requires both a political framework and an analytical framework. Both elements will be discussed in the next sections.

THE NEED FOR COORDINATED ACTION

Introduction

One of the intentions of this chapter is to explore the potential for coordinated regional-energy environment projects. Such an approach is only reasonable if there is a considerable overlap of objectives and if synergetic effects to be expected will lead to a higher performance of sectoral planning efforts undertaken so far.

It is evident that cost-saving programmes (including energy efficiency programmes) enhance the competitive position of regions, and consequently it is a meaningful policy strategy to increase regional development potential by means of smart energy savings measures and technologies. Furthermore, a more efficient use of energy resources and a lower degree of energy mismanagement is beneficial to the quality of life in such areas. It is also known from various recent studies that a favourable environmental profile is one of the primary locational factors of new-technology firms. Thus a smart regional energy policy does not only increase the overall efficiency of a regional system, but it may also lead to a more efficient use of indigenous regional development potential thus decreasing the socioeconomic gap between various regions.

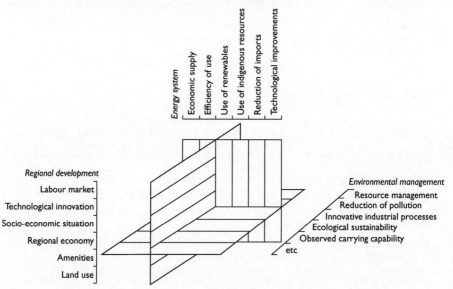

Figure 3.1 Interacting issues and objectives of energy planning, regional development planning and environmental management

The search for overlaps and synergy can be presented as a three-dimensional system of intersecting topics and objectives (see Figure 3.1). One plane in this three-dimension picture contains the most relevant objectives of energy planning, another one the issues (or objectives) of regional development, and a third one high priority topics in environmental management. Some aspects of this schematic picture will be discussed on the following pages.

Sectoral objectives

A focused policy favouring sustainable cities requires clear and well defined objectives. The following list of objectives seems to be relevant in the light of the current planning practice:

- objectives in **energy** planning:
    - low-cost supply;
    - efficiency of use;
    - use of renewables;
    - use of indigenous resources;
    - reduction of imported energy;
    - technology improvement.
- objectives in **regional** planning:
    - labour market;
    - technological innovation;
    - socio-economic welfare;
    - regional development;
    - amenities;
    - land use and physical planning.
- objectives in **environmental** management:
    - effective resource management;
    - reduction of pollution;
    - restructuring of industrial processes;
    - ecological variability.

Clearly, such objectives need a precise definition in any specific context of urban or regional policy.

Interdependencies between objectives

The objectives mentioned above are by no means independent from one another. Some typical interdependencies between energy policy objectives and regional policy objectives can be illustrated by viewing some interesting examples of recent regional energy planning:

- The success of regional development plans occasionally depends on the availability of indigenous resources: if there were no abundant sun and wind available on the Greek islands, a regional energy plan for the Cyclades could not have focused on indigenous energy sources.

- If there were not a surplus of liquid manure and low quality firewood in some German agricultural regions, a regional development plan for the Oberpfalz would have been a much less useful exercise.
- The leading position of the Danish wind turbine industry would not have come into being without the scarcity of fossils fuels and an abundance of wind energy in Denmark.

Some typical examples of interdependencies between energy policy and environmental policy objectives are:

- The objective of efficient energy use is directly related to the environmental objective of effective resource management.
- The environmental objective of reducing pollution is highly dependent on priorities in energy policy regarding improved energy technologies and efficiency of energy use.
- The objective of reducing energy demand is synergetic to the ecological and regional objective of rationalizing the use of energy.
- The objective of employing indigenous energies such as recycling waste, recovery of heat and so on is contingent upon the ecological concept of reducing the level of material cycles, since all conversion, transportation, use or deposition of materials pollute the environment in one way or another.

Finally, there are also close mutual connections between regional policy objectives and environmental policy objectives:

- Regional development requires a good environmental quality, as the latter is conditioning to a large extent the attractiveness profile of an area.
- The achievement of a favourable level of quality of life needs financial resources which usually have to be generated at the regional level.
- A neglect of environmental quality conditions may have serious implications for human health at the local level, so that these externalities mean a threat to regional development objectives.

Having sketched these interdependencies among the three classes of main objectives, it is evident that we also need a set of scientific tools for analysing co-evolutionary policy strategies oriented towards the achievement of sustainable urban development. In Chapter 4 various analytical methods will be described, but by way of illustration we will briefly mention here a variety of practical methods often used in integrated regional energy–environmental planning. These approaches include:

- market potential assessment models (focusing on the demand side);
- material-balance models (in terms of volumes or economic values of flows);
- engineering models;
- energy-flow models (in terms of energy contents);
- input–output models at local, regional and national scales;

- integrated environmental models (in terms of a wide spectrum of different environmentally-relevant variables);
- integrated process/product analysis;
- dynamic stock-flow models (in terms of the evolution of a complex ecological system);
- evaluation models (in terms of policy judgement of conflicting options);
- technical and economic feasibility models.

Design principles for such models are, among others: systems analysis, multiple-layer design, satellite-core design, and super-modelling (see Brouwer 1987).

For some regions in Europe, comprehensive causal diagrams of pollution technologies and pollutants based on computer-aided path analysis have been constructed. Some interesting empirical illustrations will be offered later in this book.

EXAMPLES OF REGIONAL ENERGY–ENVIRONMENTAL PLANNING STUDIES

In the context of this chapter, three concise case studies will be presented, each of them explicitly taking account of environmental aspects in regional and local energy planning. These case studies were carried out by the Berlin Senate (Berlin), COWI Consult (Virum) and LDK Consultants (Athens).

Case study: Berlin-Neukölln, Germany

A computer model carrying out all steps of a comprehensive energy-environment study has been designed for Berlin-Neukölln. Figure 3.2 shows a typical computer output describing all flows of waste water in the district concerned. Similarly, all paths of SO_2, NO_x etc caused by energy processes or by industrial processes have been traced from their origin to their respective disposal points. The computer model is based on the notion of a mathematical state of equilibrium of the flow system. This allows for the introduction of policy measures (ie a disturbance of the equilibrium) and for a quantitative analysis of the impacts of policy measures. This model is essentially a typical example of a materials balance model.

Case study: Cyclades, Greece

The Cyclades Regional Energy Plan takes up the issue of environmental impacts of energy production, conversion and use. Apart from a detailed analysis of impacts of renewable energy sources (geothermal, wind, solar, biomass), it focuses on air pollution caused by the use of traditional energy carriers in the transportation sector, in electricity production as well as in mining and quarrying.

One of the results of these analyses is a pollution flow diagram linking energy uses, energy technologies and types of emission (see Figure 3.3).

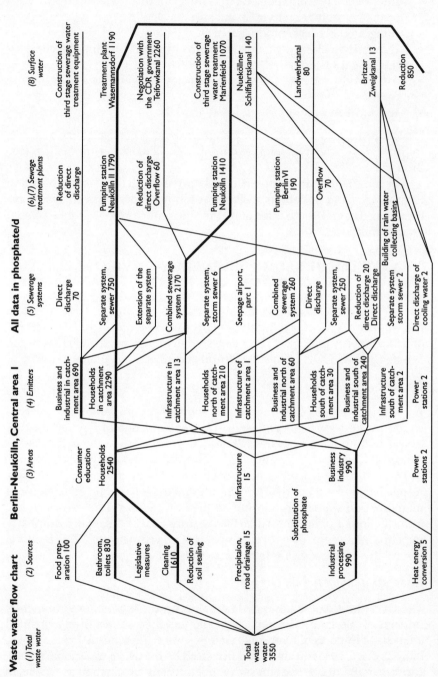

Figure 3.2 Phosphate flow balance for Berlin-Neukölln

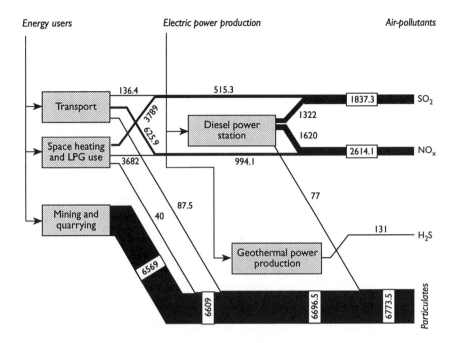

Figure 3.3 Analysis of air-pollution emissions in the Cyclades (tons)

The approach is similar to methods used in the model for Berlin-Neukölln. A computer model was not required here, because the flow analysis is limited to four major pollutants (SO_2, NO_x, H_2S and particulates), whilst the sequence of causes and effects are easy to understand.

Case study: Storstrøm, Denmark

Regional energy planning for the county of Storstrøm has dealt with alternative technical options for an expansion of the local district heating system. A computerized model is used in this case study for a comparison of technical options with regard to their impacts on:

- environment;
- energy resource balance;
- national economy (including imports);
- consumer sector;
- cash flow for municipalities, counties and state;
- labour resource balance.

The logic of the model is shown in Figure 3.4.

All these studies have been empirically applied and have provided the necessary information for sustainable development planning by local authorities.

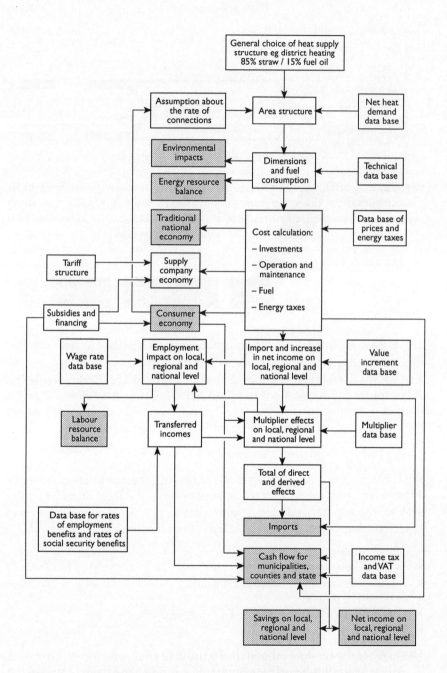

Figure 3.4 The logic of a computer model used for regional energy planning in the county of Storstrøm

DESIGN OF AN OPERATIONAL FRAMEWORK FOR REGIONAL ENERGY PLANNING

The process of economic, energy and environmental planning involves a series of interdependent steps, most of which are required for optimal decision making by market participants like industry, utility companies or energy users. The results of these steps are mainly directed at an improved understanding of causes and effects.

Some of the results of the planning process are indispensable for a consistent regional energy, economic and environmental policy; they address primarily the regional administration, that is, policy-makers responsible for an improved coordination of decision-making processes in a regional energy, economic and environmental context.

Environmental impacts of energy systems do not only depend on the respective energy carriers but also on the technologies of extraction, transportation, conversion, distribution and final consumption. The analysis of impacts will therefore have to be based on an energy balance linking technologies applied to their energy inputs and outputs.

Within this framework, a series of tools for integrated impact analysis has recently been developed, most of them having specific qualities and advantages. An attempt to synthesize experience with these different tools has led to the design of a general impact model which covers most of the topics of interest. The structure of the model and a prototype application for environmental impact analysis will be described here. The appropriate format of a technology-related energy balance (see Figure 3.5) consists of a series of balance matrices: matrix *columns* depict technologies; matrix *rows* depict types of energy. The following set of seven matrices may then be distinguished in our so-called **cascade model**:

- energy extraction technologies;
- energy transportation technologies;
- energy conservation input;
- energy conversion output;
- energy distribution technologies;
- final energy conversion input;
- useful energy output.

In the first step the respective seven matrices are established and linked into a cascade of technologies and related types of energy (see Figure 3.5). The resulting cascade of matrices represents a complete energy balance *including all technologies applied* in the chain of extraction, conversion and use.

The individual matrices are indispensable for a correct assessment of impacts, because impacts will differ for each combination of energy carrier and conversion technology. An assessment related to energy carriers only or to technologies only would, therefore, not be realistic.

The second step concerns a quantitative assessment of impacts by means of **impact coefficients**. For this purpose each of the seven matrices has to be multiplied with a corresponding matrix of impact coefficients (see Figure 3.6). For example, the conversion input matrix will be multiplied by a matrix of SO_2 emission coefficients in order to arrive at total SO_2 emissions for this part of the energy balance. Similarly, total NO_x, CO, CO_2, CnHm emissions and other environmental impacts such as land required, water used etc are computed using a separate matrix of coefficients for each type of impact

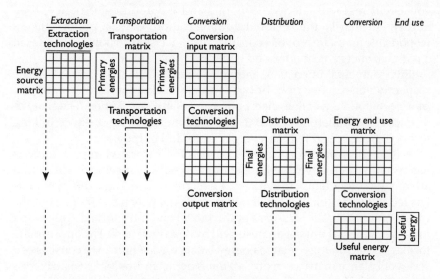

Figure 3.5 Energy balance converted into a cascade of technology matrices

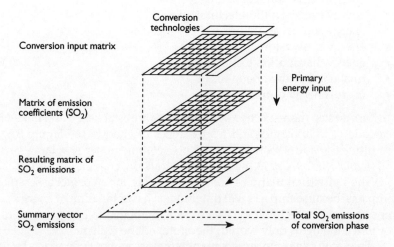

Figure 3.6 Computation of total SO_2 emissions for one of the matrices using emission coefficients

and each step of the cascade. The emission coefficients contained in the matrices can usually be taken from available national or regional studies.

The result of this procedure is a series of five environmental impact matrices, one for the extraction phase, one for the conversion phase, and so on. They may be summarized in a vector of total impacts or may be evaluated separately in order to identify the most polluting processes (see Figure 3.7). This new method which has already been applied to various actual regional energy and environmental planning problems is certainly a powerful tool for a coherent planning effort.

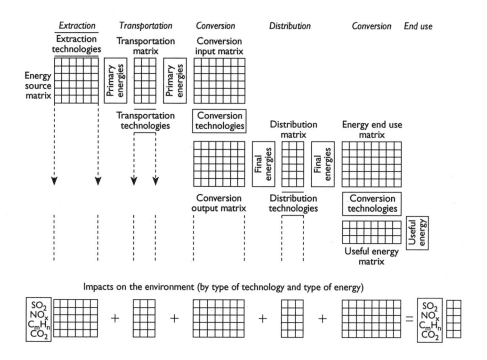

Figure 3.7 Environmental impacts computed from the cascade of technology matrices contained in the energy impact model

CONCLUSION

Integrated regional and urban energy–environmental planning using a consistent set of analytical tools may be helpful for the following purposes:

- to improve the efficiency of investments in new energy systems by helping to avoid conflicting investment strategies;
- to help to substitute ideological arguments used in public discussion

on energy systems and environmental issues by sound professional expertise;

- to guide the often much too narrow discussion of one specific pollutant in the direction of a comprehensive discussion about environmental impacts in *all* stages of the energy conversion process;
- to demonstrate that in the long run there is not necessarily a fundamental conflict between the objectives of economic growth, environmental protection and energy conservation.

Nevertheless, current practice is far from ideal. Both scientifically and politically, we still have a long way to go before the road towards sustainable development of our cities and regions is paved. Fortunately, many efforts are made in most countries to restore the balance in favour of a co-evolutionary development. In the sequel of this book various illustrations will be given of these hopeful indications. First, however, a brief overview of various analytical methods and models for energy–environmental impact analysis will be given.

4

Methods for Urban Energy–Environmental Impact Studies

URBAN ENERGY–ENVIRONMENTAL IMPACT ANALYSIS

Energy and environmental issues seem to follow the life cycle path of a normal commodity in a mature economy, characterized by phases of upswing and downswing. This also holds for scientific research in this field. And the related policy interest exhibits also the usual stages of a policy life cycle model:

1. acknowledgement of the need to formulate a new policy;
2. policy formulation;
3. realization of a solution;
4. maintenance of the solution system.

This may lead to the subsequent policy interest cycle being a derivative of the urgency of energy and environmental problems (for instance scarcity of oil, clean air or water etc; see Figure 4.1).

After the general interest in global energy and environmental issues, in recent years we observe also a wave of attention for the potential of local resource initiatives and local resource analysis. In the various phases of the policy life cycle model, the availability of and access to (energy–environment) information systems (including modelling) is a *sine qua non*.

Information systems can be used for description, impact analysis, or policy evaluation. In the case of regional or urban energy developments, they may be based on a general systems approach so as to provide a coherent framework of analysis (for example see Figure 4.2).

Resource and energy analysis has become a rapidly growing research field at the crossroads of technical and social sciences. The fourfold increase in oil prices in late 1973 and the subsequent economic crisis which has affected the industrialized world since then have stressed the relevance of designing a coherent methodology for energy and resource analysis. Despite the impressive body of knowledge regarding physical and chemical aspects

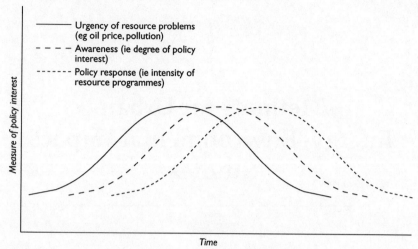

Figure 4.1 Policy interest cycle and policy response cycle as a function of resource scarcity

of energy and resource use, the overall field of energy and resource analysis is not yet satisfactorily developed (see Johansson and Lakshmanan 1985). Three major fields of energy and resource analysis may be mentioned in this respect:

1. **The exploitation and supply of energy resources**. Past experiences have clearly demonstrated the inability of many research efforts to provide reliable predictions of the stock of energy sources, depletion rates and the impacts of international politics.

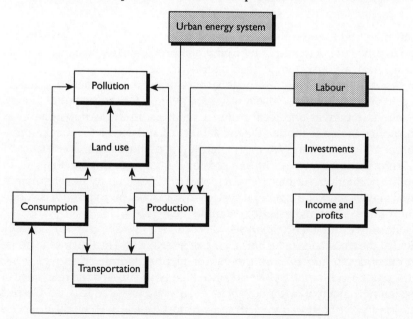

Figure 4.2 An interdependent energy systems framework

2. **The consumption of energy and resources**. The past decades have, mainly due to the oil crisis, shown a remarkable shift in energy consumption due to the increased energy efficiency of equipment in industrial installations, agriculture, transportation and households (sometimes up to thirty or forty per cent). Demand effects (for example, substitution mechanisms) are still hard to assess and to forecast with satisfactory precision.

3. **The energy technology**. In recent years, energy technology has been marked by a wide spectrum of adjustments and innovations (for example integrated heating systems, wind and solar energy). Despite the short-term inertia of energy technology, its medium-term flexibility for the design and introduction of technological innovations is remarkably high. Consequently, it is difficult to make satisfactory projections of future developments in energy and resource technology and its implications for urban and regional environmental quality.

Thus it can be concluded that energy and resource analysis is still marked by a high degree of uncertainty. Several attempts have been made to develop analytical tools that are more adequate for energy and resource analysis, both short and long term.

This chapter offers a concise review of methods/models for (local) energy analysis, paying special attention to energy technology and energy demand. The energy question is indeed a complex one; therefore the design and implementation of relevant and manageable energy policy models is a prerequisite for assessing the regional and urban environmental dimensions of energy developments. Obviously this requires large amounts of data, but unfortunately sufficiently long time series are poorly developed so that behavioural analyses are very rare. Only recently, more systematic attempts have been made to create information systems on energy issues that will serve the needs of an appropriate energy policy analysis. The majority of such information systems, however, usually address energy issues at a national level and only seldom at a regional or urban level (see Nijkamp 1983). As a result the *geographical* dimensions of spatial energy projects deserve particular attention (see also Laconte et al 1982).

The links between national and regional (or urban) energy planning are spelt out in more detail in Figure 4.3 (see Nijkamp 1985). Depicting such links requires the use of various methods and models for spatial energy and resource impact analysis which will be discussed later.

METHODS AND MODELS FOR REGIONAL ENERGY–ENVIRONMENTAL ANALYSIS

There is a wide variety of methods and models that are used for regional or urban energy–environmental analysis. They can be classified according to their purpose (for example projection, policy analysis), degree of complexity (for example small-scale models), the degree of multidisciplinarity, the time frame covered and so on. An unambiguous classification is diffi-cult to achieve. The following typology seems to cover most of the models used in current practice.

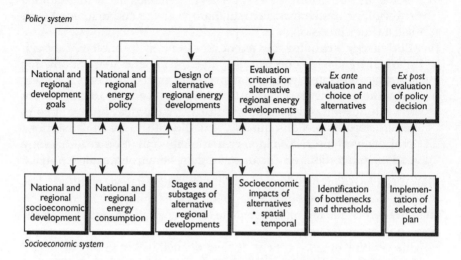

Figure 4.3   A comprehensive assessment system for energy development

Input–output models

Simple input–output methods include amongst others, the well-known E-GDP (energy-Gross Domestic Product) ratio studies. In many impact studies, regional aspects of energy and resource use are included in a broader framework of production and final demand by means of (inter) regional input–output (I–O) models (see for example Lakshmanan and Nijkamp 1980, 1983; Muller 1979).

In this way, a consistent configuration of intersectoral, interregional and intraregional production flows and related energy and resource flows can be obtained. I–O analysis is also important, since it is able to distinguish between energy use for final demand and for intermediate use. Various energy sources can be taken into account by means of an I–O framework. The same applies to environmental impacts. The dynamic I–O model at the core of the strategic environmental assessment system (SEAS) model used in the US is an example of this potential (see Ratick and Lakshmanan 1983). The model MORSE used in the Swedish case of energy planning is also a good illustration of a multiregional I–O model that provides regional-national linkages.

Drawbacks of regional I–O analysis, however, are its rigidity. In most cases I–O analysis assumes fixed coefficients because the adaptation of co-efficients due to growth, substitution and innovation is cumbersome and complicated. Secondly, I–O analysis requires large data bases, which should be adequately maintained and updated. An obvious advantage is its completeness and consistency. I–O models may be based on economic flows (ie values) or physical flows.

In order to circumvent to some extent these drawbacks, various researchers have attempted to develop similar methods that enable assessment of the gross energy requirements of products, sectors or even an entire economy. Yet the focus of these 'energy-chain' models is primarily on the level of products or product families.

Recently, this type of analysis has regained popularity. The current prominent place of environmental policies has stimulated the demand for integrative assessment methodologies (ie including the entire energy requirement embodied in all the production steps leading to a product or service). Next to I–O analysis detailed process analysis has been put forward. However, because this method often proves too laborious, as a compromise, hybrid tools have recently been developed (van Rossum et al, 1993), which use its better characteristics in an effective combination. Despite its drawbacks regarding dynamic developments, the appeal of the approach is its ability to show detailed and accurate consequences of all kinds of consumer behaviour, for example, to illustrate the difference between the choice for public transport and private car.

Energy-environmental models

Energy–environmental models serve to depict the complex interactions between energy production (or use) and the environmental implications. Examples are local air quality models and noise models. In a broader context also, large-scale models dealing with global impacts of acidification on forests, oceans etc may be mentioned here (see for example Hordijk 1991). Other, more recently developed models for climate change may be added to this list and this field has become an intensive research area in the past decade.

Energy models with substitution

The choice of inputs (including capital, labour, energy, materials) to produce a certain amount of output, based on input substitution and technological changes, can be analysed by means of trans-log substitution models (see Hudson and Jorgenson 1976; Ratick and Lakshmanan 1983; Lesuis et al 1980). These models allow for substitution by relating changes in technical coefficients to price effects, based on duality relationship between the production function and the cost function of a firm. In this way, energy input coefficients can be included as endogenous variables in models of producer behaviour, so that a system of relative factor–demand relationships can be derived. This allows for the computation of prices, substitution elasticities and changes in technical coefficients. The trans-log approach can be linked to an I–O model in a straightforward way. The substitution analysis can be carried out at two levels: one at the so-called KLEM level (capital, labour, energy and materials), and the other at the so-called intra-KLEM level (allowing for substitution between different energy components). A variety of these models depicting economy-energy relationships is part of the battery of integrated models used in the assessment of a variety of energy technologies in the US.

It should be noted, however, that both I–O and trans-log models are strongly demand-oriented, and thus have limited relevance for energy supply planning, unless they are used within a more comprehensive economy-energy systems framework.

A further application of the above mentioned class of models can be found in comprehensive (or at least integrated) econometric models (see, for instance, Jorgenson 1976). However, two major drawbacks of econometric approaches to energy analysis are:

1.   The need for detailed time series data which in most countries are only available from the 1970s onwards;
2.   The fact that most econometric models are based on a fixed structure and stable patterns, so that bifurcations or singularities cannot be taken into account very well. If lack of data precludes a valid estimation of such econometric models, simulation models may be used. Such models may be extremely helpful in case of a lack of reliable data, but also have several weaknesses:

     -   the statistical accuracy of such models is normally – from a methodological viewpoint – very limited;
     -   the data input for such models is often based on unjustified behavioural assumptions.

Apart from trans-log substitution models dealing with substitution between inputs, we may also have models focusing on substitution among energy carriers. Such models may also be cast in the framework of computable general equilibrium and vintage models.

Comprehensive regional energy system models

Comprehensive regional energy system models aim to portray regional economic and energy flows in a coherent way (see Chatterji 1980). They may be broken down into various modules:

*   an activity sub-module (including *inter alia* sectoral production and employment levels);
*   an energy sub-module (including *inter alia* various regional energy supply and demand categories);
*   a socioeconomic sub-module (including *inter alia* housing market and demographic patterns);
*   a financial sub-module (including *inter alia* public tax rates and revenue systems);

- an environmental sub-module (including *inter alia* pollution levels, damage costs and quality-of-life indicators);
- a spatial sub-module (including *inter alia* transportation and land use variables).

Another good example of a comprehensive demand-oriented approach is the MEDEE model (see Chateau and Lapillonne 1979). This was a cornerstone of the International Institute for Applied Systems Analysis (IIASA) long-term energy study (Haefele 1982) (see also the section on page 49). Such comprehensive models reflect potential information requirements, and may be based on econometric modelling techniques, I–O analysis, mathematical programming methods or simulation methods. Energy demand models, like MEDEE, are also often used in combination with energy supply models (for example MESSAGE or EFOM). Such models have also extensively been applied in the electricity sector in various regions of the US.

Energy circuit models

Energy circuit models have been developed by ecologists who aim to bridge the gap with economics. The main philosophy is that energy is an important common denominator in all ecosystems (Odum 1976), and may henceforth be regarded as the joint currency for ecological 'housekeeping' (accounting). This approach assumes that the source and quantity of available energy largely determines the pattern of functional and developmental processes in a region. Therefore, insights into the energy structure and processes of regional ecosystems are of major importance in understanding the properties and implications of regional ecosystems.

Ecosystems can, then, be linked together by means of energy flows. Such energy circuit models are extremely helpful for judging the energy efficiency of a city or region, as well as the growth in energy consumption. Many of these are simulation models based on a systems approach. Applications of such models to energy-based urban and regional planning and land use problems can be found in Costanza (1975) and Odum (1976).

A further illustration of such models can be found in network models, which are much broader in scope. These may deal with network layout and utilization optimization, choices among competing networks, energy exchange via linked networks, and environmental impact assessments at local or regional levels.

Cartographic energy–environmental analysis

The spatial dimensions of energy supply and demand can be taken into account by means of so-called cartographic energy methods or heat maps (see Allaert et al 1980). This approach is based on a computerized system that allows the user to produce detailed maps (even at a scale of 1:500) for supply and demand of various energy categories. By means of such refined grid systems, one can obtain detailed insights into the energy supply and demand of residential and industrial activities. The spatial orientation of cartographic analysis is very appropriate for analysing the geographical aspects of energy systems (for example the agglomeration advantages from district heating, energy efficiencies from locally integrated energy supply systems).

Cartographic energy analysis can also describe the energy intensity of supply and demand at any desired spatial scale and in each time period. Consequently, it allows for a permanent monitoring and comparison of energy supply and demand, so that bottlenecks can be identified and overcome by planners. At present, geographic information systems (GIS) offer the same potential, and their use in public infrastructure management is rapidly increasing. Such GIS systems and models allow also for spatial and environmental conflict analysis in connection with physical planning, public security legislation and so on (see Fischer and Nijkamp 1993).

Regional energy scenario analysis

Given the complexity and future uncertainty of energy systems, a wide range of scenarios have been constructed for the design of a feasible and consistent picture of energy supply and demand patterns. Such scenarios do not predict the future, but rather provide a meaningful image of it that can serve as a frame of reference for policy choices. A good illustration of the use of energy scenarios can be found in WAES (1976). In general, scenario analysis aims at designing a limited set of consistent future developments of a complex system, with particular emphasis on changing trends in public policies or external (global) developments (see also Hafkamp 1984). Such analyses usually have a strong policy relevance, as they are able to demarcate the range of feasible policies and their impacts on the long-term dynamics of the main features of a complex system. Clearly, scenario analysis also has a major disadvantage, as it is only based on plausible or feasible future directions, without providing a statistically sound behavioural justification. It should be added that scenario analysis can also be combined with econometric and simulation models.

Many energy scenarios, however, do not include a clear regional dimension. Regional energy scenarios may be based on three kinds of changes in the energy system:

1. Shifts in exogenous circumstances not controlled by either the national or the regional government (for example sharp reductions in oil supply by OPEC countries).
2. Policy measures taken by the national government, but not controlled by the regional government (for example a uniform national energy tax system).
3. Policy measures taken by the regional (or sub-regional) government (such as district heating system design). A regionally decentralized energy policy may increase the efficiency of an energy system, because more detailed aspects of regional land use, transportation flows, and residential and industrial locations can be taken into account.

A good example of a regional energy scenario analysis can be found in Foell (1980), who designed a large-scale regional scenario including *inter alia* four scenario properties (socioeconomic structure, lifestyles, technology and environment), and five modules (socioeconomic activity, end use energy demand, energy conversion, environmental impacts, and preference and decision structures). These were then converted into a set of operational models. On the basis of alternative assumptions regarding the scenario properties the effect of alternative input data for the energy study could then be assessed. For the preference and decision module, multi-attribute utility theory was a relevant tool. In general, such scenario experiments may be very helpful tools in scanning the future and in tracing uncertainties and bottlenecks at local, regional, national or even supranational levels.

Multidimensional energy policy models

Policy analysis for energy systems may be either *discrete* or *continuous* in nature, dealing with distinct alternatives or an infinite choice set respectively. An example of a discrete energy evaluation system can be found in Blair (1979), who analysed various alternative regional supply systems using conflicting criteria such as energy costs, environmental quality and conservation of natural resources. The preference analysis was based on Saaty's prioritization method (by means of an *eigenvalue* analysis). In addition, various compound scenarios were created to resolve policy uncertainties regarding energy issues.

Examples of continuous multidimensional energy policy models can be found in Lesuis et al (1980) and Hafkamp and Nijkamp (1983). The latter study is based on a comprehensive, large-scale, multiregional and multisector I–O model including energy and pollution. Three conflicting objective functions were considered: employment, environmental quality and energy security. The compromise strategies in this model were based on an 'ideal-point' approach. A recent survey of such multidimensional evaluation models can be found in Nijkamp et al (1990).

Having now provided a brief overview of some relevant methods and models for local and regional energy and resource analysis and planning (with the main emphasis on the demand side), we will now examine a specific class of **comprehensive** energy models in more detail. These have proven to be suitable tools for local energy analysis, the so-called MEDEE models.

MODULAR DESIGN FOR COMPLEX ENERGY SYSTEMS

In the present section a conceptual model for medium- and large-term energy analysis will be presented based on the so-called MEDEE framework (see Chateau and Lapillone 1979). This model is one of the major tools used by the Commission of the European Community (EC) to explore systematically the uncertainties regarding technology and demand for energy in the member states. The model has also been used in other countries (for instance the US), while it has also played a role in the international energy study carried out under the auspices of the IIASA (see Haefele 1982).

The MEDEE model is based on a detailed and integrated analysis of the energy demand determinants in a country, and a sophisticated scenario of its economic, spatial and social developments. It aims at identifying various end use categories, the socioeconomic needs and the (spatial) economic activities creating energy demand for various modules, as well as the relationship between sub-modules that describe their evolution in the medium and long term. The medium- and long-term horizon has been chosen in order to forecast energy consumption over a time period that is long enough to take into account technological adjustments (for instance, construction time for new energy production facilities or equipment), and to prevent demand forecasts from being affected by ad hoc influences. The design of the MEDEE rests upon an integration of systems analysis and scenario analysis, complemented with either econometric or simulation models. A simplified, conceptual version of this model is represented in Figure 4.4.

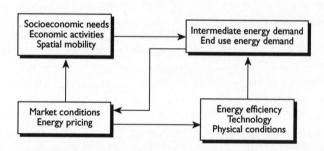

Figure 4.4 Conceptual version of the energy demand model

Next the MEDEE model is operationalized by using the following steps:

- A disaggregation of energy demand (right upper block of Figure 4.4) into a set of coherent modules (industry, households, etc).
- A closer examination of energy demand determinants in each module (ie the impacts exerted on the right upper block by the remaining three blocks) and of relationships between these modules.
- Development of a simulation model by formalizing the relationships within and between modules, and by linking the sub-modules on the basis of the first step.

Altogether the MEDEE model may be regarded as both an engineering and an economic model, thus requiring both detailed technical spatial and socioeconomic data. It has a hierarchical modular structure made up of ordered sub-modules and recursive equations. The output of the model is given in terms of final energy demand distinguished according to users and end use categories. A quasi-operational structure of the MEDEE model is given in Figure 4.5.

The operational version of the MEDEE model consists of estimated or calibrated relationships describing the evolution of energy demand as a result of changes in socioeconomic conditions, spatial activity patterns, economic activities, behavioural adjustments and technological progress. In case of lack of data, simulations may be carried out, while wild fluctuations are prevented by imposing plausible upper and lower limits on the functioning of the system. In the operational version, three type of variables are distinguished:

1. Endogenous quantitative variables (determined by the internal mechanism of the model itself).
2. Exogenous quantitative variables (assumed to be known prior to the prediction of annual values of the endogenous variables).
3. Qualitative and quantitative scenario variables (describing the main trends of technical, political, social and economic determinants of the system at hand).

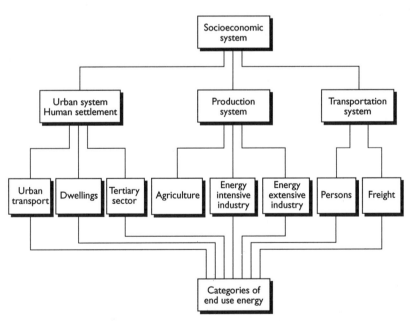

Figure 4.5 The main structure of the MEDEE model

In the case of **qualitative** variables, so-called tabular functions are used in order to transform qualitative scenario indicators into quantitative values in a consistent manner by means of ordering statistics. Each of the three modules (urban system/human settlements, production system, transportation system) will now be represented briefly in Figures 4.6 – 4.8. It should be noted that this schematic representation of the modules is still a drastic simplification of the actual model structure which is based on numerous sub-modules.

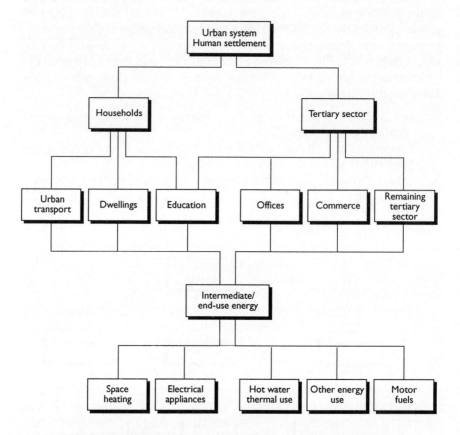

Figure 4.6 The urban system/human settlement module

The advantage of the MEDEE model is its flexibility, since it can easily be adjusted to specific economic, spatial or technical conditions in a certain region or country. Nowadays the computer package which is available allows the user to select or to suppress certain (sub) modules according to his or her own needs.

In addition to the modular design of MEDEE, it is important to pay more specific attention to the scenario approach implied by this model. A scenario aims to represent the main future tendencies of a system in a plausible and consistent way. Examples are trend and contrast scenarios. The scenario approach in MEDEE is governed by a triple-layer structure:

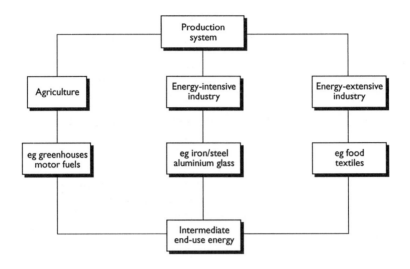

Figure 4.7 The production system module

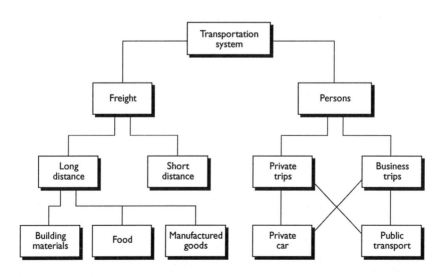

Figure 4.8 The transportation system module

- **World scenarios**: characterize the international environment of the system and the economic/political relationships between the system and its environment (growth of the world economy, international labour division, etc).
- **Socioeconomic scenarios**: characterize the main economic, social, political and technological features of the development of the (national or regional) system at hand (urbanization, technology, social policy, etc).
- **Modular scenarios**: characterize exogenous evolutions of the various individual modules (for instance sectoral innovation patterns).

The qualitative and quantitative information obtained from these scenarios is used in each relevant layer of the modular structure of the model. The information may be obtained directly from policy makers or generated by experts (for instance, by means of *Delphi* techniques). Given the modular pattern of MEDEE, the formalization of all relevant relationships (either by means of econometric or simulation methods) and the scenario information, one may generate – on the basis of a set of input data on socioeconomic and energy variables – a wide variety of energy demand results for the medium- and long-term horizon of the system under consideration. Clearly, the MEDEE approach also has some limitations, such as a strong demand for consistent scenarios containing very detailed economic, technical and behavioural information.

The MEDEE approach is very well suited for distinguishing between homogeneous energy demand sectors, because of the hierarchical, modular structure of the model. As far as spatial differences in the development of sectors influence energy demand, spatial distinctions are to be made in order to obtain homogeneous sub-sectors, as is the case in the MEDEE model with respect to the urban system. If necessary or desired, this may be extended to other parts of the model.

A complete regionalization is also possible by specifying the variables for the regions or cities taken into account. The estimation of the development of the regional variables may be derived from the national structure by a top-down extension of the national–regional variables. For a national model like MEDEE however, several hundreds of values are already required for the data base. This number will be much higher if many of these data have to be specified for, say, four or five regions or cities. Many of these data may not be available and consequently have to be synthesized. Furthermore, for the construction and pre-recording of the tabular functions, many reports and experts have to be consulted.

The MEDEE model as such may also be applied to a region instead of a country. In such a case, problems with data availability may also exist. On the other hand, modules not necessary for the region concerned can easily be suppressed, and others may be extended. However, in such a case it seems to be wise to create a new, region-specific model, using the MEDEE approach (and if desired the so-called SMASS software, which is used for the MEDEE model). In this case, the model can be specified in relation to the specific energy demand structure of the region, the relative weight of the energy demand sectors in the region, as well as the data available. An application to the Dutch region of Westland can be found in Nijkamp and Tiemersma (1985).

CONCLUSION

It is evident that a diversity of analytical methods and techniques may be used in urban energy planning. They range from computerized local energy information systems or detailed urban energy flow balances to formal mathematical, econometric models or sophisticated evaluation methods. Several of these methods have already been tested and applied at the local level. It has become clear from such experiences that these methods are extremely important tools for energy and environmental planning aiming at urban sustainability.

5

Energy Policy and Urban Sustainability

URBAN ENERGY–ENVIRONMENTAL PLANNING: A NEW FOCAL POINT

In the previous chapters a broad outline of the potential of urban energy and environmental policy analysis has been offered. We asserted that a combined urban energy–environmental policy is a potentially powerful vehicle for achieving the goal of urban sustainability. Such a policy is in agreement with the general aims of energy policy as formulated by the European Community. In the past years, the European Community has formulated various general objectives in regard to energy policy, with the following aims:

- increased energy efficiency;
- less environmental pollution caused by energy use;
- reduced energy costs for the business sector;
- increased spending capacity of households through a reduction of energy costs in the residential sector (with a simultaneous improvement of living conditions);
- less dependence on foreign (or extra-regional) energy sources;
- enhancement of regional growth through effective energy planning.

The achievement of these results needs a wide variety of different policy measures, most of them being a responsibility of national, regional or local governments. Urban energy planning is one of such policy initiatives. It aims at contributing to the fulfilment of the above mentioned general results, although from a decentralized point of view the focus is much more on the *potential* of urban areas to support these objectives. There is evidently a wide variety of urban energy problems and related urban energy and environmental policies. Some of them have failed, but as we will show in this book, several of them have been relatively successful. Apparently there is a need for a further exchange of good experiences in the area of urban energy–environmental planning.

Cities are the workfloor of operational planning in many respects, such as transportation, environmental quality management, physical planning, energy provision, social planning and so forth (see Solomon 1980). Decentralized policy initiatives at city level – which cover at the same time a considerable share of the population of a nation – may increase planning efficiency (see Rogner 1984; Thabit and Stark 1985). Urban energy–environmental planning may be a good case in this context. It should be realized, however, that in general urban energy–environmental policies are multifaceted and linked to various sectors in the city (such as physical planning, transportation, housing, land use, environment etc). Such policies have a higher chance of being broadly accepted by all parties involved if they are directed towards generating benefits for almost all sectors: industry, electricity companies etc. Thus a 'multi-client' orientation of urban energy–environmental plans is an important way of enhancing its successfulness. Such a multi-client orientation presupposes an integration – or at least coherent treatment – of different sector plans in a city (such as housing planning, dwelling insulation, district heating, waste management, industrial cogeneration, heat recovery at an incineration factory etc).

Urban sustainability policy – induced by energy–environmental policy – is not a uniform recipe for each city. Specific urban energy and environmental policies differ widely. In the next three sections we will outline briefly some prominent examples of such policies, namely district heating, industrial cogeneration, and conversion and load management of electrical power.

URBAN DISTRICT HEATING

District heating refers to any energy system where heat resulting from another source (such as electricity generation and combustion of fossil fuels) is distributed to the domestic sector for heating purposes. By using waste heat the same amount of final energy use can be reached with less primary energy and at lower environmental costs. Clearly, the capital-intensive nature of district heating may make it rather costly, but in general this can be compensated by the decline in energy costs (Wene 1987). Of course, the economic feasibility of CHP (Combined Heat and Power) technologies depends also on the price level of fuel to be used by CHP companies.

The idea of CHP is relatively simple (see Rüdig 1986). The heat waste in thermal power stations is very high (generally about 60 per cent). CHP technology consists basically of tapping the steam when it leaves the steam turbine, leading the steam through a heat exchanger and thus heating water that can be provided to households or industries via a network of pipes forming a district heating system. This technology is already fairly well established. It was used in the late 1880s in the US and Germany, while nowadays it can be found in many countries such as the UK, Scandinavia, Austria and the Netherlands.

Overall the energy savings from district heating are rather significant. According to Rüdig (1986), there is a long-term saving potential of 26.34 to 38.87 *mtoe/year* in the EC as a whole. Although technically feasible, this impressive amount, however, has not yet been achieved. The central problem is not technical but social: there is a wide variety of economic, behavioural, organizational and political obstacles to the adoption of such energy conservation technologies. It turns out that in many countries the organization of the energy utilities in particular is detrimental to the broad penetration of district heating. More especially, the centralized structure of the electricity supply industry in some countries often impedes a widespread adoption of CHP technologies. The problem is that district heating systems are operated mainly by municipal electricity companies, so that the large centralized electricity companies regard CHP often as a threat and are not eager to cooperate. Thus the divergence of interests at an institutional level has sometimes reduced the rapid spread of district heating. Moreover, in existing residential areas there is often already a fully fledged network for the provision of natural gas (or in some cases like in France, electricity). Switching to a new heat supply system in such areas would imply very substantial depreciation costs with regard to the replaced network as well as the heating systems of each dwelling. Therefore, the introduction of district heating has far better opportunities in new residential areas (or in older residential areas designated for reconstruction in the framework of urban renewal).

In addition to the above mentioned barriers, existing tariff schemes are able to create a – sometimes artificially – unattractive financial context for the development of district heating systems.

INDUSTRIAL COGENERATION

The CHP technology described above can also be used for industrial purposes. In fact, urban areas usually have a fairly dense industrialized pattern and it is no surprise that the use of waste heat for industrial purposes has gained much popularity. According to Verbruggen and Buyse (1986), cogeneration is a good case of economies of scale where the costs of generating outputs – electricity and heat – in a combined way is lower than the costs of generating outputs separately. Also in the field of industrial cogeneration it has to be realized that such systems are operating on a limited heat market and a broad and strong power market, so that competition between these two systems may be detrimental to cogeneration, unless the cost advantages are evident. Industrial cogeneration can, however, also take place within the industrial plant or between industrial plants, so that a private organization of CHP systems is easier to establish.

In general, a cooperation between utility companies and decentralized energy supply systems is most advantageous. In a study by Becht and Zijlstra (1985) an extensive analysis has been made of the potential of such systems for the densely populated province of South-Holland in the Netherlands. By using different scenarios (such as regarding the share of coal in electricity production, institutional reorganizations, price level of oil etc), the authors conclude that a significant part (approximately 20 per cent) of the energy demand in the area concerned can be met by means of CHP systems. In particular the industrial energy demand in the Botlek area near Rotterdam could benefit from the application of cogeneration, especially because in this area cogeneration has already found an extensive application (mainly in the oil refinery and chemical industries). We conclude also that the emission of pollution (notably SO_2 and NO_x, as well as thermal water pollution) will decline considerably. We believe that the success of cogeneration will be determined to a large extent by institutional rearrangements between the large public utility companies and the decentralized cogeneration units.

A special type of industrial cogeneration – not based on a CHP system – may be a system were urban solid waste is centrally collected and burnt, while the resulting waste heat may be delivered back for industrial purposes or used for electricity generation. Such recycling systems have gained much popularity in recent years, especially in larger cities such as Rotterdam and Amsterdam. Apparently in the area of urban energy and environmental management there are various possibilities for more efficient and clean technologies which have yet to be investigated.

CONSERVATION AND LOAD MANAGEMENT PROGRAMMES

In recent years an increased interest in conservation and load management programmes of utility companies has emerged. Efficient load management may be very cost effective, especially because the planning of peak load capacity is very expensive. In order to avoid average over-capacity and to spread excess demand more evenly, conservation and load management programmes may be very appropriate vehicles. Such programmes depend of course on time scheduling of activities in both the industrial and the household sectors. In Perrels and Nijkamp (1988) an operational model for load management in the Netherlands has been developed (see for full details Perrels 1992). Clearly, effective load management requires detailed insight into the allocation of time of consumers and producers, and into ways of influencing such patterns (for example by means of price policies). Such information may be based on individual survey data, energy audits, electricity billing data and so on. An example of the structure of an energy load management study can be found in Figure 5.1 derived from Hirst (1987).

A remarkable success with regard to load management in households and greenhouses has been achieved in the Westland area of the Netherlands. The voluntary installation of direct control devices on washing machines and growth stimulating illumination in greenhouses had a significant impact on the reduction of peak loads. The combination of a customer friendly approach with a rate reduction created easy acceptance among households and greenhouse farmers (see van Oortmarssen 1987; Schieke 1987). Furthermore, it should be noted here that much research on load management has been carried out in the US (see *inter alia*, Sexton et al 1987; Train et al 1987).

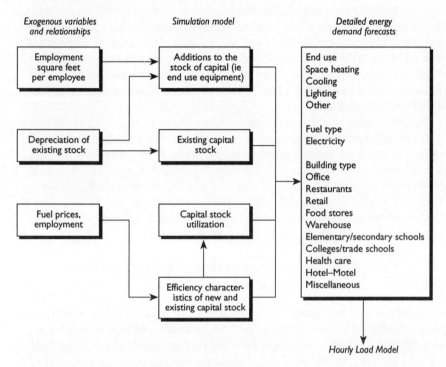

Figure 5.1 Schematic diagram of disaggregated commercial energy end use forecasting model

It is evident that such energy conservation and load management programmes require very detailed demand forecasting models as well as detailed insight into alternative regulatory treatments of such programmes by public utility companies. Nevertheless the economic benefits of such programmes are likely to be very high, so that further analysis of the potential of such programmes in urban areas is certainly an important research issue.

THE CITIES PROJECT

The European Community (EC) has recognized the above described need for decentralization of the implementation of energy and environmental policy schemes. From 1983 to 1988 the Community has developed a programme to support regional and local energy studies in all member states. These studies served to provide a more efficient energy planning framework for their own region as well as an example to other regions. However, it was felt that in many circumstances the implementation of energy measures might preferably be further decentralized toward the local – notably urban – level. Therefore the Directorate-General Energy (DG XVII) of the Commission of the European Communities defined a new programme aimed at the support of energy programmes in cities.

In order to be able to demonstrate the potential of such urban energy–environmental policies, twelve European cities have been identified and invited to collaborate in a cross-European urban energy–environmental initiative. This is the so-called CITIES (Community Integrated Task for the Improvement of Energy-Environmental Systems in Cities) project. It focuses on a non-exhaustive but interesting set of European cities with a remarkable energy–environment policy initiative. These twelve cities, one from each member state of the EC, agreed to participate in a comparative urban energy survey and to provide active policy support for the fulfilment of these goals. In alphabetic order these cities are:

Amsterdam	Gent
Besançon	Mannheim
Bragança	Newcastle
Cadiz	Odense
Dublin	Thessaloniki
Esch/Alzette	Torino

The aim of the CITIES project was to identify interesting examples of successful urban energy–environmental policies (serving also environmental objectives) in order to disseminate this information and knowledge to a broad set of other European cities which also would like to develop sustainability strategies.

As part of their task, each of these cities has produced a systematically structured report focusing on promising results of urban energy–environmental policy in the city concerned. The present section will list only the main items that were encountered in the individual city reports.

The reports of the twelve cities appear to endorse various other publications on energy (*inter alia* Europlan 1988; Lundqvist 1989), that the following urban energy–environmental policy areas appeared to feature prominently:

- urban energy supply systems;
- urban waste management;
- urban transport systems;
- information, communication and marketing;
- management of the municipal capital stock;
- the development of integrative urban energy concepts.

Each of the cities involved has concentrated on two or three items from the above list. The results from the various reports will be presented in a concise form in Part B of this book; more details can be found in a background report (see EC 1991). Finally, Part C will offer an interpretation and policy analysis of these findings.

For the time being, it suffices to mention that it is very encouraging that an increasing number of cities actively show their concern for the improvement of the local energy and environmental situation. Even if the national institutional framework concerning energy is sometimes unfavourable for local initiatives, cities are clearly willing to explore the possibilities of developing a decentralized urban energy–environmental policy favouring sustainable development of the city. Although various urban energy initiatives are undeniably positive, they touch at the same time the heart of urban energy planning, ie *institutions*. Clearly, other aspects such as citizens' participation, are important as well, but an appropriate institutional framework is a prerequisite for a city to establish a comprehensive urban energy and environmental policy. It should, however, also be recognized that the actual organization of urban energy supply cannot be captured in one common or uniform design for all European cities. National, regional and local differences in, for instance, economy, social order, local politics or climate may necessitate tailor-made organizational structures. Before focusing on such policy questions (see Part C), Part B will first present some interesting information and lessons collected from various European cities participating in the CITIES initiative.

PART II

ENERGY AND URBAN ENVIRONMENT IN EUROPE:
IN EUROPE:
A COMPARATIVE OVERVIEW OF
TWELVE CITIES

6

Amsterdam

THE NATIONAL ENERGY SITUATION

The Dutch energy scene is dominated by natural gas, which covers about 50 per cent of the primary energy supply. The high penetration of natural gas for various applications and in all sectors was an explicit goal of the national energy policy in the sixties and seventies based on the large Groningen field. Since the oil crisis in the mid-seventies the involvement of the national government in the energy field has increased. Originally attention focused on diversifying primary sources and improving energy efficiency of equipment, buildings and vehicles. The diversification strategy included *inter alia* substantial shifts in the shares of primary sources used for power generation. This meant in particular more coal and virtually no oil, while the nuclear debate is still inconclusive.

The improvement of energy efficiency was supported by means of more strict standards, higher subsidies, more information campaigns and so on. The introduction of district heating (DH) often gave rise to a lot of difficulties due to the privileged position of the natural gas grid as well as to inadequate planning. Particularly successful was the National Insulation Programme (NIP) which aimed at the improvement of dwellings. In connection with this programme, as well as with a national improvement programme for older (rented) dwellings, 30,000 dwellings in Amsterdam were insulated while another 15,000 were both renovated and insulated. On average, energy consumption appeared to drop by some 30 per cent after insulation. Rent increases associated with the insulation costs are generally lower than the decreases of energy costs.

Recently, the national energy policy received a new impetus from increasing environmental concerns. The National Environmental Plan (NMP) has specified goals for emission reduction for SO_2, NO_x, and the like and a stabilization of CO_2 emission in the year 2000. Consequently, energy saving has become a very important element in the national energy policy. In addition, local authorities and utilities have initiated or will initiate energy action plans.

THE ENERGY SITUATION IN AMSTERDAM

The Amsterdam economy is strongly service oriented (trade, finance, transport), and consequently the energy intensity of the local economy is relatively moderate. The residential sector is the largest consumer category, followed by transport. About 80 per cent of energy consumption is from natural gas, mainly for space heating purposes. The use of oil products is virtually limited to the transport sector.

Dutch cities have a range of instruments that may be used in their energy policy. Some of them relate to decentralization and local detailing of national plans such as for housing and physical planning. Other vehicles exist, because the municipality controls the local companies for energy distribution and public transport and parts of the public building stock.

Recently the Dutch utility sector has been reorganized. As a result the local power generation companies merged into larger regional companies, while so-called horizontal integration has realized local energy distribution companies which cater for gas, power and district heat (if present). Moreover, local distribution companies are allowed to install small power units and to buy from remote suppliers. In Amsterdam the enlarged local policy space is used to achieve peak cutbacks, to promote renewable energy sources and to save on electricity and natural gas. These energy saving activities are an integral part of a larger Environmental Action Plan of the Amsterdam municipality. The Energy Company Amsterdam (EBA) has established a department for new energy plans.

EXAMPLES OF IMPLEMENTED ENERGY PROJECTS

The EBA is implementing a programme for the installation of small scale combined heat and power units (CHP). Allowing a maximum pay back time of eight years, projects totalling a capacity of 150 mw were identified. The current plan stretching over 15 years foresees the installation of 100 mw CHP. The typical locations of the units are hospitals, large apartment blocks, pensioner homes and some large public buildings. Thus a broad spectrum of established dwellings can be covered.

A special project is the installation of an 38 mw expansion turbine, which is based on the difference in pressure between the main gas transport grid and the local grid. This concept is expected to set an example to other Dutch local energy utilities, especially to those where CHP has not yet drawn sufficient attention.

The EBA successfully promoted the use of energy saving bulbs in households. The energy companies of Amsterdam and The Hague negotiated a special price for the energy saving bulbs with several electric bulb producers. Furthermore it agreed with the local retailers on an effective way to distribute the bulbs. About 150,000 bulbs were sold, causing an estimated reduction of annual electricity consumption of 11 GWh – a considerable amount for a medium-sized town

In order to help low income households to reduce their energy bills, a special task force (the E-Team) has been established. The E-team officials act on the request of clients of the EBA. First, an exploratory visit to the client will be made in order to trace the likely cause of a high energy bill (such as behaviour, bad equipment, poor insulation, etc). The client is then given advice and very low cost measures may be implemented. If more costly improvements are necessary, a financial scheme is discussed with the client. For the non-Dutch speaking clients information translated in a foreign language is available.

PROSPECTS

For the next few years the intended policy has been formulated in the Amsterdam Environmental Action Plan. The plan contains proposed actions with regard to soil, water, air, waste management, traffic, physical planning and energy. As regards energy, various plans have been formulated by the Energy Company Amsterdam aiming at the reduction of energy use by the introduction of combined heat and power units, the use of waste heat of electricity power plants, the promotion of energy savings among customers and the improvement of the energy quality of new homes.

7

Besançon

GENERAL OBSERVATIONS

Since 1974, independence of supply has been one of the main objectives of France's energy policy. The French Agency for Energy Management (AFME) is a decentralized organization with regional divisions throughout France. It plays a fundamental role in implementing French energy policy and is an active partner in a wide range of initiatives designed to reduce energy expenditure and consumption and to promote renewable energy sources.

French city authorities have no direct responsibility for such matters, and conventional energy sources are distributed exclusively by the national energy utilities. But city authorities are actively involved in the management of their own buildings and facilities; they are directly responsible for certain public services; and urban planning is part of their basic mandate. Thus there is some scope for decentralized initiatives. The city of Besançon has played an active role here.

In the past few years Besançon has focused its energy–environmental policy on:

- heating cost control;
- air quality surveillance;
- urban public transport.

These issues will now briefly be discussed.

ENERGY AND PUBLIC BUILDINGS AND FACILITIES: HEATING COST CONTROL

The following heating cost control initiatives and achievements are noteworthy:

- Besançon's city authorities commissioned a full audit of heating quality, heat production and distribution equipment in more than 400 public buildings.
- 90 per cent of the oil-fired heating installations were converted to natural gas, which were cheaper and generated less pollution.
- The 'centralized technical management' approach has made it possible

to optimize overall operation of the heating system. A remote management system is used to control heating plants in line with technical requirements and to deal with equipment failures, while at the same time an attempt is made to pinpoint energy waste, control costs and generate detailed energy consumption reports.
- Steps were taken to improve the heating efficiency of public buildings. Generators were installed to provide the largest energy consumers with an independent electricity production capacity. Special equipment was installed for more rational use of electricity in lighting applications.

ENERGY AND ENVIRONMENT: AIR QUALITY SURVEILLANCE

The following observations can be made:

- Road traffic is largely responsible for Besançon's pollution problem.
- The atmospheric pollution detection system installed in the 1970s has now four measurement stations in strategic points around the city, each of which uses 10 pollution identifiers/analysers for specific pollutants.
- Managed by an independent association, the detection system is soon to be linked up to France's central monitoring network and will be one of the sources for the nationwide atmospheric pollution data base.
- The city authority's efforts to improve the energy efficiency of its buildings and facilities have halved CO_2 emissions and brought a tenfold reduction in SO_2 emissions in ten years.

ENERGY AND THE TRANSPORT SECTOR: PRIORITY TO PUBLIC TRANSPORT

Besançon has also developed an active transport policy:

- Since 1974, public transport has been given priority in the city's traffic plan in an effort to overcome congestion and pollution in the city centre.
- Buses are used for 22 per cent of trips in the city and are the most common single form of transport in the city centre (35 per cent of all trips). Besançon is an exception in France in that public transport availability is 70 per cent higher than the national average for cities of comparable size. The number of trips per year per inhabitant is twice the French average.
- This strategy has had a significant impact on the city's energy expenditure: a bus consumes five times less energy per person than a private car. Total energy consumption by the public transport system is 2250 toe/year, which is equivalent to an average of FFr 0.36 per passenger.
- In view of the increase in road traffic since 1985, the city's new policy involves extending the coverage of the public transport network and

undertaking various major infrastructure projects to improve traffic flows.

Besançon's energy–environmental objectives for the coming three-year period are as follows:

- Stabilizing results of space heating initiatives.
- Launching a multi-year project to reduce electricity consumption, starting with public lighting.
- Consolidating the global energy/environment approach (integration of energy management with plans to reduce pollutant emissions).
- Developing relations with other European cities to share experiences and views on energy issues.

In conclusion, Besançon has set some realistic targets in achieving its energy–environmental goals.

8

Bragança

THE NATIONAL ENERGY SITUATION

The energy situation in Portugal is one of double dependency: imports cover more than 80 per cent of the country's primary energy, while oil alone represents more than 70 per cent of the needs. Large hydro installations and biomass are the only two national sources of energy of some significance. The valorization of the endogenous potential is today one of the primary concerns of the Portuguese Government's energy policy together with external supply diversification and the improvement of energy system efficiency.

THE LOCAL ENERGY SITUATION

The mainland of Portugal is subdivided into 18 counties. The city of Bragança is the capital of the Bragança county and is located in the North Region of Portugal. The municipality covers an area of 1174 km², has a low population density (about 30 inhabitants/km²) and is the only urban centre of the county with more than 10,000 inhabitants (25,000 in 1989). The agricultural characteristics of the county – small farms with low productivity as well as relatively low standards of living – turns the city into the central focus for the overall development of the region.

The climatic conditions of the north eastern region create a considerable need for heating (2405 degree-day (base: 18°C)), most of which is not satisfied, or if satisfied, is not officially accounted for in the energy balances, since this need is mainly met through non-commercial wood burnt in fireplaces or ovens.

As in other Portuguese regions, data on local energy consumption is scarce and inconsistent, due to the lack of a reliable energy accounting system at a disaggregate level. Nevertheless, the existing data on final energy consumption show that the transport sector is the most significant (64 per cent) while the industry represents only 4 per cent of the total use of energy. Thus Bragança is not a typical European city

In 1989, electricity consumption in the municipality of Bragança was 37,856 mwh, where the importance of the domestic sector (42 per cent) and the high level of consumption in the city of Bragança (21,010 mwh) should be emphasized. In 1988, regional consumption of liquid fuels totalling nearly 60 kton (including LPG) represented 0.9 per cent of the total consumption in the mainland of Portugal.

EXAMPLES OF IMPLEMENTED PROJECTS

The physical geography of the region is very favourable for the implementation of hydroelectricity plants. In addition to this potential, there is a need to irrigate agricultural regions allowing a multiple use of water reservoirs. In 1988, the publication of the Independent Producer Regulation, establishing the legal framework for energy production from power plants with less than 10 mw as well as for the grid connection, led the municipality to design several projects in order to exploit the hydro potential of the region. In this respect, the financial support provided by EC through the 'Energy Demonstration Projects' and 'VALOREN' Programmes allowed the development of three projects with special interest for the region.

With the financial support provided by the Demonstration Programme, the town council of Bragança, in cooperation with AFME, designed and constructed a small hydro power plant at the Gimonde site. This project, besides producing 515,000 kwh average per year, is an important showcase for the demonstration of this energy technology, both in the region and in Portugal as a whole.

The VALOREN Programme contributes to the operation of Alto Sabor's hydro-power plants, which have the following objectives:

- electricity production at two power plants: Montesinho and Prado (total installed power: 5500 kw);
- reinforcement of Bragança's water supply;
- irrigation of agricultural land;
- development of tourism.

Besides the income from selling the electricity produced (estimated at 17.4 gwh/year), these projects will also generate non-energy benefits of a high importance for the population, namely higher living standards and an improvement in regional development.

PROSPECTS

Other actions of special interest for this region include:

- The utilization of biomass for the production of heat and hot tap water. The production of heat using agricultural and forestry by-products is currently being implemented in the county, in a hotel, a hospital and several school buildings. Some of these projects will be financed by the VALOREN Programme;
- Analysis of the public and private buildings' thermal needs. This study conducted in the form of an inquiry in the city of Bragança, involves the town council and a local consultancy agency;

- Analysis of the solid waste management at the council level. The aim of this project, which will be conducted by the Regional Association of Municipalities, is to evaluate the energy valorization of the municipal waste and to contribute to the solution of environmental problems.

The efforts made by Bragança's town council were focused on the development of endogenous energy resources and because of energy expenses at the local level. In common with many other municipalities, the lack of local energy experts and the secondary importance of energy problems are the chief barriers to the implementation of an efficient and integrated use of local energy resources. However, Bragança is a good example of a small city located in one of the less developed Portuguese regions and financially supported by EC programmes, that tries to exploit its endogenous potential.

9

Cadiz

GENERAL OBSERVATIONS

Cadiz is situated in the south of Spain in the Andalusian region. It has an average population of 150,000 inhabitants, fluctuating between the summer and winter seasons. It may be regarded as a medium-size town in the Spanish context, with quite some potential for urban energy–environmental policy.

The local administration is responsible for the organization of public services such as transport, solid waste, water supply, street lighting and electricity supply and distribution (via its special public agency, SMAES: Servicios Municipalizados de Agua, Electricidad y Saneamiento).

Cadiz is fed by the national electricity system (132 and 62 Kv) of the 'Sevillana de Electricidad'. The tension is transformed to 28 Kv, then 6 Kv and finally 220 v. The number of subscribers fluctuates between 62,000 and 63,000. There are 5000 light points in the streets.

In the present chapter only two urban energy–environmental initiatives will concisely be dealt with: photovoltaic power and sewage treatment.

NEW ENERGY–ENVIRONMENT INITIATIVES

Regarding the alternating current, Cadiz' Council is currently undertaking some research on the feasibility of implementing solar photovoltaic power. This done in two small pilot projects. One of the studies is devoted to refrigeration of fresh milk, the other to hotel business equipment.

The hotel business installation was carried out in the 18th century district, a place of artistic and historical interest. This electric photovoltaic power supplies now all restaurant services (lighting, refrigeration of drinks and smoke extraction) with a 112 photovoltaic modulus and 4700 Amp/h battery equipment. These small scale initiatives turned out to be fairly successful, so that at the level of a medium-sized town realistic energy policies can apparently be put in operation

Cadiz has also a preprocessing plant where the water is automatically roughed-down, degreased and cleaned. It is then pumped by means of a marine emission pipe to the Atlantic Ocean. As it is physically impossible to build a purifying plant for the sewage, an Association of Municipalities of the Bay of Cadiz has been formed to establish and manage the treatment and later use of the sewage in industrial applications.

INSTITUTIONAL ARRANGEMENTS

The management and organization of the environmental and energy services in Cadiz are undertaken on the basis of common operations, for example, administration, commercial operations, control and checking, computerization and so on. A computer department is in charge of constructing all application packages such as the turnover of electricity, water, sewage or waste. The technical office designs and directs the necessary investment works related to water and electricity. The commercial department accomplishes the new connections after a contract for the delivery of water and electricity has been signed by the customer. Also the bills and debts are automatically administered. The direct benefits of this system are efficiency, accountability and centralized management.

10

Dublin

NATIONAL ENERGY POLICY IN IRELAND

Prior to the first oil price crisis in 1973, national energy policy in Ireland focused on ensuring adequate supplies of cheap oil imports, and on developing indigenous energy sources, mainly peat and hydro. In 1978, oil accounted for 75 per cent of total fuel utilization. Since the 1979 crisis, national energy policy was directed towards reduction of dependence on imports, and diversification from oil as well as allowing free competition between fuels in order to maximize consumer choice and minimize costs. In 1979, the government instituted the National Energy Conservation Programme, which had nationwide coverage.

As a result, reliance of final energy consumption on the national level on oil had, in 1986, been reduced to 49 per cent, with coal (18 per cent) the next important source, followed by electricity (14 per cent), peat (10 per cent), and natural gas (9 per cent).

Residential heating which accounts for about 75 per cent of residential energy use has, with the housing stock having grown from 740,000 units in 1971 to over 1 million units in 1986, remained at a level of 33 to 35 per cent of national energy use, despite improvements in insulation and heating appliance efficiency. Based on predominantly rural traditions in Ireland, solid fuel has remained the heating source in more than half of Irish homes. Gas still accounts for less than 10 per cent, and many homes do not yet have central heating. Consequently, smoke concentration and sulphur dioxide content have been a major problem, particularly in the densely populated Dublin region.

DUBLIN AND ITS RESIDENTIAL ENERGY CHARACTERISTICS

The Dublin city region with a population of (1986) 921,000 represents 26 per cent of the national total, and covers an area of around 300 km². It is administered by three local authorities – Dublin Corporation, Dublin County Council, and Dun Laoghaire Corporation – which have geographically complementary roles. These roles, however, do not include ownership or management of energy supply utilities. Rather, the energy responsibilities of these authorities have been confined to the management of energy use in their own premises and facilities, and to managing the environmental consequences arising from the government's national energy policy.

Total final energy consumption in the Dublin region in 1986 is estimated at 1.7 million TOE, including 1.4 million TOE of direct fuel consumption with local pollution effects. The sectoral breakdown of these uses is estimated at 30 per cent each for residential buildings, industry, and transportation, and 10 per cent for commercial and institutional buildings.

Dublin has had a low level of market penetration by oil and gas in the residential sector, and practically no district heating. About 300,000 out of the 350,000 tonnes of solid fuel consumption – two thirds of the total heating sources – were high-volatile bituminous type coals with high smoke emission characteristics.

DUBLIN'S AIR POLLUTION PROBLEM AND RESOLUTION PROGRAMME

While in the late 1970s monitoring of atmospheric concentrations of sulphur dioxide and smoke revealed a steady downward trend, a significant rise of daily incidences of excessive smoke concentrations has raised growing concern. This problem seems to be particularly acute in more disadvantaged residential areas, where low-cost, bituminous type coal tends to be the main fuel source with more than 90 per cent of the market. Generally, this fuel is burned in open fireplaces where the conversion efficiencies range from 45 per cent down to 20 per cent (for fireplaces without a boiler, the most common type). Moreover, many city dwellings still lack even rudimentary thermal insulation measures.

Due to the large number and diverse characteristics of buildings, and the socioeconomic structure of consumers, addressing the problem by means of official administrative measures proved to be difficult. In this context, the 1980 EC Council Directive on air quality proved to be of vital importance. While a network of monitoring stations recording smoke particulate and SO_2 concentrations had already been established, the Directive determined internationally accepted limit value requirements to be complied with by 1993, and future guide values that are significantly more stringent.

Arising from the EC Directive, the Air Pollution Act 1987 was passed in Parliament, which provided the Minister for the Environment and local authorities with new powers and obligations. As a result, Dublin Corporation was in a position to institute an array of measures which included:

- monitoring air quality under Air Quality Regulations based on the EC Directive;
- establishing Special Control Areas where only authorized fuels – gas, fuel oil, low smoke solid fuels, electricity – or authorized burning

appliances may be permitted;
* administering financial assistance to owners or occupiers of premises in Special Control Areas to contribute to the necessary investment in fuel conversion: in 1989/90 the Minister for the Environment provided £5 million for this purpose.

In addition, various technical and publicity measures were taken, partly in cooperation with or in delegation to other agencies.

CONCLUSIONS

Based on 1989 performance, it can be estimated that by the end of 1991 more than 100,000 new natural gas installations would have been set up in the Dublin city region. The decree by the Minister for the Environment in January 1990, that the sale and distribution of bituminous coal in the Dublin city region would be prohibited as of October 1990, will further this development. A fundamental strategic measure planned for the near future is the development of an Air Quality and Energy Management model for the Dublin city region, designed as a tool for facilitating and evaluating decision making in this policy area.

11

Esch/Alzette

NATIONAL ENERGY POLICY

The fact that Luxembourg is almost exclusively an energy consumer and not an energy producer obviously reduces the number of opportunities for optimizing energy production in comparison with other European countries. However, this in no way rules out the possibility of national initiatives being taken which make for considerable improvements in the sector of energy distribution and local energy consumption.

Guaranteed energy supply and gradual reduction in energy dependence are the two essential targets of energy policy and will in the future result in intelligent use of available resources in Luxembourg. The main characteristics of this policy are as follows:

- energy saving in private and public buildings;
- greater use of combined heat and power;
- specific energy saving through measures to improve the public transport system;
- promotion of new and further developments in the field of renewable sources of energy.

The Luxembourg Ministry for Energy has emphasized its intentions by offering state subsidies for the installation of the energy-efficient plants. The Ministry for Energy has set the tone by its involvement in the company LUXENERGIE, which, together with other partners, will construct district heating plants on the Kirchberg Plateau.

A first plant with 6100 kw thermal and 720 kw electrical power will be followed by a large number of others, so that district heating will have a broad geographical coverage.

The establishment of an energy agency will make it possible in future to undertake exhaustive research in Luxembourg in the fields of:

- new energy technologies
- renewable sources of energy
- rational use of energy.

It can certainly be said in conclusion that Luxembourg's energy policy has embarked on a change for the future which will not only optimize energy production but also make for a long-term improvement in the environment.

DESCRIPTION OF THE ENERGY SITUATION IN ESCH

Esch currently has a population of 25,000 and is the second largest town in Luxembourg. Of its total area of 1435 hectares some 528 hectares are built up with around 6000 buildings. The number of vehicles amounts to 10,700. For years natural gas (currently 38.7 per cent) has been making serious inroads into fuel oil (currently 40.7 per cent) as regards the primary energy used.

Electricity consumption in 1989 was as follows:

day	55,620,000 kwh
night	18,000,000 kwh

The growth rate over the last ten years averaged about 2 per cent a year.

A NEW ENERGY COMPANY

The company SURRE, which was founded in Esch in 1988, consists of shareholders from four different branches. Its main task is to pinpoint projects for the construction of district heating plants, to examine their viability and to provide turn-key production of the plant. By selling the heat and power produced, the aim is then to achieve economic amortization of the investments made. In this context SURRE is keen to make a considerable contribution to economic and social development at the regional level.

LOCAL ENERGY CONCEPT

The district heating plant at the Brill School at Esch was the first project undertaken by SURRE. In this project three individual building complexes are supplied with heat and the electricity produced is fed into the public grid.

The plant arrangement is as follows:

1 district heating gas engine	358 kwt and 210 kwe
1 district heating diesel engine	365 kwt and 400 kwe
2 heating boilers	600 kwt
Total power	*1323 kwt*

The diesel engine is also used to supply emergency power to the local theatre, which in addition is linked up for heating purposes. Given a maximum operating period of around 16 hours a day, about 2,600,000 kwh heat and 1,200,000 kwh power will be produced each year.

The local pollution emission will be reduced as follows:

Particulate 70%	NO_2 25%
CO_2 45%	SO_2 75%

The use of primary energy will be reduced by 32 per cent.

After the planning phase had been completed in November 1988 the plant went on stream in December 1989. On the power production side the plant makes a considerable contribution to reducing power peaks in the town power supply network. The total investment channelled into the construction of the plant amounted to ECU 631,430, which corresponds to a specific investment per kwe of ECU 1052. Given a lifespan of 15 years, the internal rate of return is 19 per cent, which, for a known capital contribution of ECU 163,700, is a positive economic result.

There is further potential in Esch in buildings where combined heat and power plants can be installed. A second district heating plant is currently being installed in another school complex. The results of these two plants will provide a sound testimony and encourage development of the idea. Successful use of available potential, however, will depend to a large extent on national policy decisions in the energy and environment sector.

CONCLUSIONS

The aim of the first district heating plant in Esch is to demonstrate that this technique can be used not only for its ecological advantages, but is also feasible from a technical and economic viewpoint.

Given a positive outcome, the company SURRE and the Esch administration are determined to play a pioneering role in the field of non-polluting energy production.

12

Gent

THE NATIONAL ENERGY SITUATION

In the case of electricity and oil products, the supply of energy at the national level is mainly a private sector business while the supply of natural gas and the import of coal is managed by national public enterprises. Yet for electricity generation and oil products public interventions also exist, particularly concerning strategic planning and minimum and maximum price levels.

Endogenous coal production, which is to be phased out within a few years, comes under the responsibility of the Flemish government. Also regarding energy research, the three regions of the Belgian federation are responsible, instead of central government. Together with France, Belgium has the highest share of nuclear energy for electricity generation. Natural gas is imported from the Netherlands, Algeria and Norway.

THE ENERGY SITUATION IN GENT

The economy of Gent is based on its seaport facilities and the heavy industry attracted by these facilities. As regards natural gas, households are the largest consumers, taking about two-thirds of the natural gas supply. In the electricity sector the non-domestic users (offices and industries) are more prominent consumption categories. Though oil-based space heating still exists, the use of oil products is concentrated in the transport sector and a few heavy industries (as a switching fuel). District heating is used in a few large public facilities.

The end use prices for electricity and natural gas are fixed by a national committee, and consequently the municipality has little influence on this part of the energy situation. Since 1981 local generation and distribution have been separated. Generation is now organized on a national basis, while the distribution in Gent and adjacent areas (Flanders) has a regional–local structure.

Since 1981 public buildings have to be heated according to ministerial guidelines. Also in 1981 the city of Gent established a so-called 'Energy Cell'. The Energy Cell functions as a kind of municipal steering committee aiming at the promotion of efficient energy use in municipal buildings as well as stimulating and monitoring energy savings projects. The Cell also publishes an annual report as part of the municipal budget proposals. Thus increase of public awareness is a major vehicle of energy–environmental policy.

For external consultation the municipality has installed an Energy Counter, which is an information centre to the citizens about possible energy efficiency measures at home.

EXAMPLES OF IMPLEMENTED PROJECTS

Gent has quite an extensive programme regarding waste management. It includes:

- a municipal waste processing plant with a composting and an incineration section;
- a network for separate collection of glass, paper, motor oil, tyres, construction materials, biological waste and mercury batteries and thermometers;
- a dry anaerobic conversion installation (DRANCO) producing biogas, which in turn is used to generate electricity. Thirty per cent of the electricity is used by the DRANCO installation itself; the solid by-product, a kind of compost, is sold on the market.

Gent has a district heating system amounting to 28 mw in 1988. The system caters for about 1000 dwellings, 4 hospitals, 4 offices, a school and a sports complex. Thus, in principle, considerable areas with existing buildings can be covered

Various buildings owned by the municipality (schools for example and sports facilities) have been fitted with energy optimization equipment. These computerized systems which control the heating and lighting systems take into account how and to what extent the building is used over the day as well as the influence of the actual weather conditions (temperature, sunshine, wind, etc). Savings on annual consumption of natural gas and fuel oil amount to 22 per cent in schools. Optimization equipment has also been fitted in swimming pools, resulting in a reduction of 30 per cent on natural gas consumption and in a reduction of 10 per cent on electricity during the day and of 23 per cent on electricity during the night. The installation of similar optimization equipment in other municipal buildings has been planned.

PROSPECTS

Plans for the present decade (1990–2000) focus on waste management and energy efficiency. In most cases these plans are integrated in strategic plans for the entire Flemish region.

In general, standards and requirements concerning waste and waste processing have become much stricter. Moreover, prevention of waste production and reduction of the volume of waste have become important new policy goals. The 20 existing waste incineration plants in the Flemish region will be replaced by five new incineration plants producing electricity, of which one is in the Gent area.

As regards investing in energy efficiency, it should be noted that local authorities are in a difficult position due to budgetary procedures. In practice these disencourage heavy investment in renovation, energy efficiency and so on. Some changes in budgetary procedures would facilitate the establishment of investment flows aimed at energy savings. However, despite these institutional impediments many energy investments have been undertaken and will be undertaken in the future in and around the city of Gent.

13

Mannheim

NATIONAL POLICY BASIS FOR ENERGY SUPPLY IN GERMANY

As a consequence of the increases in energy prices in 1973, the goals of energy policy for the Federal Republic have, in the same year, been reformulated by government. Focal points of the energy programme have since been:

- economical use of energy;
- reduction in the use of oil through an increase in the supply of other available energies;
- stable supply and optimal use of locally produced coal;
- expanded supply of natural gas;
- increase in the use of district heating;
- consideration of ecological necessities in every energy supply strategy.

ENERGY SUPPLY IN THE MANNHEIM REGION

Mannheim, a city of 300,000 inhabitants, is the main centre of one of the most important agglomerations in south western Germany, the Rhine-Neckar region, with a total population of 1.8 million. Out of the 171,000 persons employed, 49.3 per cent work in manufacturing, 50.7 per cent in trade, transportation and other services.

Energy supply in the Mannheim urban region falls under the responsibility of Mannheimer Versorgungs- und Verkehrs-Gesellschaft mbH (Mannheim Utilities and Transport Ltd). As a holding, this company is fully owned and controlled by the city, and holds ownership of three corporations that deal with the fields of utility production and procurement, supply and distribution to customers, and public transport.

Excluding the field of transportation, the primary energy use of 9400 million kwh relies mainly on coal (62 per cent). Major contributors are also natural gas (20 per cent), and oil (15 per cent). Solid business and household wastes, now contributing 3 per cent, are of growing importance as an energy source. Final energy consumption relies almost equally on electricity, district heating and natural gas (26 to 25 per cent each), oil (18 per cent) and coal (5 per cent).

THE MANNHEIM INTEGRATIVE URBAN ENERGY CONCEPT

Urban energy policy in Mannheim is guided by the Integrative Urban Energy Concept of 1983. This concept states as its main objectives:

*   cost and price conscious supply of final energies to consumers and business;
*   securing appropriate energy sources in the long run; and
*   contributing to the environmental quality of the urban region.

Among the instruments that are applied toward these goals are:

*   application of a pricing system that covers costs, and allows for a financing of investments to secure future productivity but avoids excess profits;
*   utilization of all possibilities to save energy, and substitute solid and liquid primary energy;
*   expansion of supply systems for district heating and natural gas heating;
*   support of acceptance of these systems through advertising, information and financial assistance to customers;
*   management of energy resources through the use of cogeneration, thermal treatment of waste, and the utilization of side-heat; and
*   minimization of emissions through technical provisions of highest standards.

LOCAL ENERGY PROJECTS

District heating

In Mannheim, the first efforts to establish a district heating system date back to 1938/39. In 1977, based on a study commissioned by the Federal Ministry of Research and Technology, and supported from federal funds within the nationwide Programme for Investments in the Future, the Stadtwerke Mannheim initiated their district heating demonstration project. Across the urban area, district heating preferred areas were determined, based on topographic and transportation-related criteria, the density of heating demand in a particular area, the age structure of existing supply systems, the new or renewal investments necessary etc. Thus economic and ecologic characteristics are most important.

Consequently, in district heating preferred areas, appropriate duct systems were installed and existing supply systems for other heating energies such as natural gas, dismantled wherever possible. In order to create a favourable response to the system, consumers were offered not only information and advice, but also financial contributions toward their investment outlays for new appliances. From the point of view of the supplier these subsidies proved economical where they made the dismantling of parallel energy supply systems possible.

Under this policy, during the period 1984–1989, granting subsidies of DM 1.7 million allowed investments of DM 9.7 million to be waived – investments which would, otherwise, have been necessary. As a result of these policy measures, today 38.3 per cent of all residential units and 26 per cent of total demand for final energy in Mannheim are supplied with district heating.

Thermal waste treatment

A major heating and power producing station, Heizkraftwerk Nord, began operating in 1964, using a combination of solid waste, natural gas, and oil for cogeneration of district heating and electricity. In 1988, the oil input had been reduced to about 15 per cent. The percentage of energy produced from wastes in the total supply of final energy in Mannheim is now 3 per cent of the electricity, and 18 per cent of the district heating.

Emission of toxic gases and particles from this installation has been drastically reduced since 1983 as a result of various measures:

- technical optimization of incineration procedures;
- reduction of sulphuric content of oil inputs;
- transition to bivalent oil-gas incineration, and a reduction of oil inputs altogether;
- primary NO_x reduction;
- de-sulphurization of smoke-gases;
- installation of a waste-water cleaning plant;
- the installation of equipment for catalytic de-nitratization of smoke-gases will be completed and set in operation in 1993.

CONCLUSION

The case of Mannheim shows that a consequent, well-balanced, long-term energy supply policy at the local level, based on and reinforced by nationwide regulations and support systems, is quite capable of contributing to economic and ecological improvement in the local-regional energy system.

14

Newcastle

NATIONAL ENERGY POLICY

The UK energy bill in 1987 for end users was £38,500 million, equivalent to 9 per cent of GDP. The intensity with which energy was being used fell by 7 per cent across the whole economy between 1983 and 1987 and the Government estimates that in addition there are 20 per cent more savings to be made, using established conservation techniques. Over £500 million per year savings are attributed to Energy Efficiency Office Programmes, the main Governmental energy agency. Regional offices administer the 'Best Practice Programme' – advice, information and assistance on energy efficiency – and carry out audits.

THE LOCAL ENERGY SITUATION AND POLICY IN NEWCASTLE

The population of Newcastle is 286,000 and it is the centre of the north east of the UK. The annual expenditure on energy has been estimated at £1600 million, using 100,000 therms of gas and 1350 gwh of electricity. Presently the energy utilities are changing from state to private sector monopolies. These will steadily be opened to more competition, halting the high level of energy prices. Industry uses 48 per cent of electricity and the domestic sector 55 per cent of gas, with very little oil or coal used at all.

The City Council has had an energy policy since 1968, and currently has nine staff employed to reduce energy use in the City's own stock as well as in the community. The Council owns over 1000 buildings and in the last 20 years has switched energy supply from oil and coal so that now 95 per cent of their buildings are heated by natural gas. A special unit called the 'Energy Management and Information Unit' (EMIU) operates to implement Council policy for their own buildings and provide advice services to industry and commerce too. Thus a focused urban initiative has demonstrated its potential.

Commercial and industrial tariffs have decreased while domestic prices have risen with inflation. In the last ten years energy consumption has decreased by 35 per cent through technological advances, reducing reliance on oil and electricity, and improved education and training. Combined

Heat and Power projects are also increasing with, for example, a 150 mw combined cycle gas-fired plant to be completed in 1993.

LOCAL ENERGY PROJECTS

The local energy projects are mainly concerned with urban waste energy management, buildings and institutional and organizational management.

The Council has reduced the need for landfill sites and provided a cheap power source by opening a waste incinerator at Byker which produces fuel pellets. 100,000 tonnes of waste are disposed of annually, and the incinerator produces the equivalent of 5000 tonnes of coal per year. The fuel pellets are sold at £18 per tonne and used in schools and the largest district heating scheme in Newcastle.

The EMIU uses a computerized system of monitoring, targeting and analysing energy use in 1000 council buildings. A Performance Indicator (energy per unit area) is calculated and file opened for each building, so that targets of energy conservation can be met. Capital of £400,000 has also been invested in planned preventative maintenance of energy aspects of buildings.

The EMIU covers two broad areas – technological aspects and advice. The former includes the building management, fuel purchasing and tariff advice, capital investment (saving an estimated £2 million since 1980–81) and operation of the 'Auto-dial Energy Management Systems'. Advice is mainly given to domestic consumers including debt work for low income householders and simple Energy Audits for small businesses. There is also contact with exhibitions, fairs, and two local Energy Action Voluntary Groups.

CONCLUSIONS

Newcastle City Council has proved successful in the areas in which it has direct influence. It has set an excellent example in managing its own buildings, and from this is able to offer advice and demonstrations of successful building energy management. It has solved the problem of waste management and produced a commercially viable fuel for important energy users. It is nationally known for its marketing of energy conservation principles through EMIU and the voluntary agencies which it helps.

15

Odense

NATIONAL ENERGY POLICY

As a response to the new energy situation at the beginning of the 1970s, the goals for the Danish energy policy were to secure the supply of energy at the lowest possible cost and to reduce the vulnerability of the Danish energy supply system. At that time the country was totally dependent on oil imports.

The last fifteen years of planning activities have resulted in a high degree of self sufficiency based on a comprehensive reduction of the oil share in the total consumption, on oil and natural gas production from the North Sea, on an increase of the overall energy efficiency of production and supply and on carrying out a large programme for energy savings.

The recent growing environmental concern has had a decisive influence on the new nationwide Energy Plan for Denmark, published in 1990. Based on the recommendations of the UN's Brundtland report, this plan focuses on the following objectives: reduction of energy consumption, conversion of supply to less polluting sources and technologies, increased cleaning of flue gases and intensified R&D within new sustainable technologies.

LOCAL ENERGY SITUATION

In the centre of Denmark, located on the island of Funen, the city of Odense covers approximately 100 km². With 175,000 inhabitants it is the third largest settlement in Denmark. More than 60 per cent of the dwellings are single family houses. In 1988 the total heat demand was 8880 tj/year, and the total electricity consumption 735 mwh.

The major part of the energy supply is provided by a combined heat and power plant, Fynsværket, built in Odense in 1953. The present power output amounts to 574 mw with a corresponding heat output of 911 mj/s. An additional new block (430 mw and 450 mj/s) is planned to start operating in 1991.

As a result of a political decision taken by the City Council in 1979, 93 per cent of the heat demand is now covered by heat production from the central cogeneration system based on coal. Due to the high efficiency of the CHP concept district heating prices are very low (90 dkk/gj including VAT).

Almost all of the total electricity consumption is produced at Fynsværket. The annual production is 752 mwh with a consumer price of 0.95 dkk/kwh including VAT.

ENERGY POLICY IN THE CITY

The energy policy has been determined by the heat supply plan approved by the City Council in 1984. The plan has now been nearly achieved. As well as this, the City of Odense is presently concerned about ensuring a sustainable future development for the energy sector.

The local administration is responsible for local planning activities within all sectors, ie energy, waste disposal, urban planning and transportation. Furthermore, it is responsible for environmental approval of industrial plants, including energy producing units. The district heating system is owned and operated by the municipal administration. This organizational structure is of great benefit when integration of energy and environmental aspects are an important matter in the overall municipal policy.

Energy savings have a high priority for the local energy policy. Despite the fact that heat prices in Odense are the lowest in Denmark, the domestic heat consumption has been reduced by 28 per cent during the past ten years. Initiatives aimed at savings in electricity consumption have been intensified and good results have been achieved through energy management in public buildings.

Within the field of domestic and industrial waste a new treatment plant was launched in 1989 in order to intensify recycling of paper, glass and plastic and composting or organic matters.

To limit the environmental impact of urban transport the municipality decided in 1989 to introduce new 'environmental' buses having lower energy consumption and cleaner exhausts. A new structure for public transport is under consideration in the city.

SUCCESSFUL URBAN ENERGY PLANNING

The energy–environmental policies in Odense are mainly focused on district heating systems, efficiency increase in energy networks, and public service management.

By establishing new networks in the outer urban areas, 95 per cent of all potential consumers are now connected to the system. Because of the high overall conversion efficiency (85–90 per cent) of cogeneration compared to the traditional conversion efficiency of 40 per cent in condensing power plants, the extent of DH-supply has contributed to an overall annual energy saving of 1000 tj since 1979. Another consequence is the low heating prices paid by consumers.

The ongoing renovation plan for networks comprises approximately 2 x 442 km distribution pipelines in 12 areas for a total investment of 484 million dkk. The profitability of these investments is provided by energy savings in the system (saved heatloss, waterloss and pumping energy) as well as saved repair expenses.

In response to the higher energy prices in 1979 the City of Odense decided to start a process of restricted energy consumption in public buildings. Four different measures for energy management were defined:

1. registration of energy consumption;
2. heat inspection carried out by an energy consultant giving a report and proposing measures to be applied;
3. implementation and energy saving measures;
4. information.

The result of this action has been successful. A total investment of 51 million dkk during the period 1981–88 provided a net accumulated benefit of 20 million dkk. One of the main tasks now is to consolidate these results by constant control and monitoring of the energy consumption.

CONCLUSION AND PROSPECT

It appears that the predefined goals have been achieved in accordance with the objectives.

The district heating system, based on cogeneration, covers the whole city and 95 per cent of all potential consumers are now connected to the system. Concerning the energy savings goals, the energy monitoring of public buildings ensures an annual saving corresponding to 13 million dkk. Finalization of the ongoing renovation of the DH network and enhanced activities with regard to overall energy savings constitute the two main tasks to be completed in the future.

Ensuring people's needs without destroying nature and the environment is the aim of Odense City's energy policy, a policy in accordance with the Brundtland recommendations for sustainable development.

16

Thessaloniki

NATIONAL ENERGY POLICY

As a consequence of high dependence on oil products in Greece, as well as its relatively unfavourable energy efficiency, the state energy policy is designed towards the improvement in both these areas. It hopes to achieve this through intensive utilization of the indigenous conventional and renewable energy potential, natural gas penetration, modernization of public refineries, and implementation of relevant pricing and institutional policies. National energy policy is exercised by a number of public agencies and corporations, the Public Power Corporation (PPC) being the major actor and monopolizing the electricity market, while the government supervises and controls the whole energy market. The centralized structure of energy production, supply and distribution in Greece does not provide sufficient room for a thorough planning at the urban level.

QUANTITATIVE DESCRIPTION OF THE ENERGY SITUATION IN THESSALONIKI

Thessaloniki is the country's second largest conurbation, with a population of 706,180 inhabitants (1981); the Municipality of Thessaloniki itself has a population of 406,413. With a continental climate, oil holds a major share in the city's overall energy balance, and is especially used for heating purposes. Per capita energy consumed in the city is higher than the average for the country, reflecting a high industrialization rate.

QUALITATIVE DESCRIPTION OF ENERGY-RELATED URBAN PLANNING

Given strict budget limitations, Municipal authorities in Greece have limited capabilities concerning large-scale planing projects. Moreover, given that Athens absorbs most of the central authority's attention, because it is the absolute centre of the country's economic activity, the effects of insufficient policymaking for the periphery are especially felt by the country's other urban centres, where problems are increasing fast and without control. On the other hand, in contrast to other Greek cities, Thessaloniki possesses a most powerful policymaking instrument, namely a Master Plan, which is a law of the state and the only means through which local authorities may promote the development of the city. Energy is a separate feature of the Master Plan of Thessaloniki, and the relevant targets of the Master Plan chiefly concern the improvement of energy efficiency in the domestic, industrial and transport sectors of the city.

DESCRIPTION OF SUCCESSFUL URBAN ENERGY PROJECTS

The major fields that have improved in the Master Plan are urban energy supply systems, urban waste management and urban transport systems. Thus the urban energy-environmental policies appear to have a wide coverage

The short- and medium-term goals of the city's urban waste management policy include modernization of waste collection and disposal methods, adoption of economically feasible waste management techniques, implementation of correct (sanitary) landfill, and regeneration of abandoned sites. According to the conclusions of municipal researchers, the most desirable and economically feasible solution to the city's waste management problem is the installation of a waste combustion plant producing steam to be used in industry.

The city's energy supply system is quite efficient and well functioning. Energy supply systems planning in the municipality concerns mainly demand forecasting and efficient allocation of resources. An attempt at smoothing out the city's load curves has actually improved energy efficiency in space heating, but has created undesirable effects in the overall electricity consumption pattern.

The fact that transportation accounts for 26 per cent of the city's final energy consumption renders transport planning a crucial factor affecting the urban energy balance. Along with the development of the city structure, a lot of urban transportation planning attempts have been implemented, most of which were simply revisions of previous inefficient ones. Currently quite a few projects are in the pipeline, all of which aim for a radical restructuring of the city's traffic system. The projects include the construction of ring roads, a general traffic study, a study for the selection of an appropriate metro system, studies for the restructuring of bus routes, and a programme for short-term improvement of traffic conditions.

CONCLUSIONS AND PERSPECTIVES

Despite its valuable historical heritage, Thessaloniki is among the European cities suffering from severe development problems, as a result of a peculiar combination of physical and political circumstances. Both the Municipality of Thessaloniki and the City Master Plan conceive energy as a driving force for local development. City planning considerations over local energy supply systems, urban waste management and transport systems appear quite promising and are economically attractive. At present, the city has identified the origin of the problems it is confronted with, and plans a variety of interventions towards the achievement of a variety of targets. The fact that several of the basic determinants for success are missing – funds, technical back-up, etc – is recognized by the relevant city agencies which believe, however, in the catalytic action of both the Community's regional development programmes and the cooperation with leading European cities.

17

Torino

THE NATURAL ENERGY SITUATION

The urban energy policy of Torino is in accordance with the national policy objectives on energy use and supply. Energy saving is of vital importance. In this context combined heat and power generation, both in the industrial sector and for space heating purposes at the urban level, plays an important role. In this framework, a significant role can be played by the municipal energy utilities, as these can manage – depending on local situations and in differing proportions – electricity production and distribution, gas, and hot water distribution in urban areas, while they can also utilize as energy sources hydropower, fossil fuels and urban solid waste or biogas obtained from urban sewage treatment. Following a recent government decision, municipal energy companies (and also private producers) may sell to the National Utility Company (ENEL) the surplus electricity arising from cogenerative or renewable resource plants. The development of cogenerative plants in connection with urban space heating is far lower than the level in other industrialized EC countries.

THE ENERGY SITUATION IN TORINO

Torino has decided to develop a rational urban energy policy for the problem of thermal energy supply to households, services and small and medium size industrial activities. A technical team has been formed, charged by the City Administration with the task of investigating suitable solutions for energy saving programmes in the field of space heating. The industrial structure of the city leads to a high demand for energy by both industrial and domestic users. Electricity and natural gas are the main energy sources. The Torino area has fairly severe air pollution as a result of geographical conditions (low dispersion capacity of atmospheric pollution) and industrial and residential space heating practice. In recent years the urban policy of Torino has been very alert in developing energy saving programmes and clean air programmes, amongst others by focusing attention on district heating systems and on the improvement of the natural gas supply network. Also advocated is an improvement in the electricity distribution network and the street lighting system.

EXAMPLES OF IMPLEMENTED ENERGY PROJECTS

A good example of an energy success story in Torino is the development of district heating poles with combined heat and power plants. Three districts in Torino, Le Valette, Mirafiori Nord and Torino Sud, have implemented a heating network leading to significant energy savings, especially where this network was linked to combined heat and power generation. In this context, the previously mentioned technical team has played an important role.

The improvement of the natural gas supply network is also worth mentioning, as the increase in natural gas consumption – coupled with the practical disappearance of coal and oil and with the reduction of gas oil – have exerted a significant positive impact on air quality. An important element in this respect has also been the intensive effort devoted to the pipe and fitting renewal.

PROSPECTS

The urban energy policy programme of Torino comprises various elements:

- New programmes, namely monitoring air quality conditions and developing strategies to keep critical traffic situations under control;
- continuing existing policies regarding the district heating poles in Torino (including intensified efforts to stimulate R&D and design activities);
- construction works serving to create post-combustion equipment;
- R&D and design of a planning model aimed to provide the right tools for a comprehensive interpretation of the system.

Various new planning initiatives for effective urban environmental and energy strategies are also foreseen, such as the following:

- the validation of the atmospheric dispersion code through reliable experimental data (especially when particular meteorological conditions prevail);
- the visual impact arising from plant and network integration into the urban structure;
- the necessity of studying the evolution of the market share between district heating and natural gas direct utilization, combined heat and power production and heat pump utilization;
- the electricity exchange with the National Electricity Board, within different tariff perspectives.

PART III

INTERPRETATION AND POLICY ANALYSIS
OF THE CITIES PROJECT

18

A Retrospective Interpretation of the Cities Results

INTRODUCTION

Efficient energy use and related environmental management constitute nowadays a massive challenge to technology and policymaking. Effective energy and environmental policy is necessary in view of the global problems of the burning of fossil fuels and the loss of vegetation which – as a result of the accumulation of carbon dioxide in the atmosphere – contribute to the greenhouse effect. At the same time awareness is growing that cities may be key players in solving problems related to energy consumption.

Cities have always played a prominent role in the histories of our cultures and societies. As large-scale towns and cities grow, their capacity to sustain and regenerate themselves will need to grow at an equal if not greater pace. Towns and cities in the western world will probably take the lead in this regeneration process and may, therefore, provide feedback and learning examples for planning processes adopted in developing countries. Feedback is also needed for prompt networking of 'best practices' among established urban areas. This forms also the background of this book.

It is realized increasingly that modern cities are facing severe problems. At the root of the challenge lies the need of existing urban areas and growing cities for a decision-making machinery which enables them to contribute to a sustainable development of both the developed environment and the natural environment.

Consequently there is a need to develop and maintain an up-to-date picture of the variety of processes that are taking place and to intervene if necessary and whenever possible. While large-scale or global forecasts provide a useful overview, they take a long time to generate and tend not to contain the necessary detail that can be achieved from monitored history of more manageable case studies. Neither will forecasts and planning studies produce results on their own. Only decision makers, whether in business or as consumers, can really take the actions that will be necessary to support their own well-being. The dissemination of knowledge and technology will be crucial to success, an example being the results of the above mentioned CITIES project, which serves to cope with the negative externalities of modern urbanization and to regard cities as the challenge for a more sustainable development.

CITIES AS ISLANDS OF SUSTAINABILITY

Especially in our era, urbanization has become a worldwide phenomenon. Urbanization presupposes an intricate and efficient organization of space and time for all human activities. Mainly due to the division of labour, mankind has managed to benefit significantly from economies of scale in geographical concentrations. Especially after the introduction of mechanized production (leading to industrialization), large scale concentration of human activities – and consequently urbanization – became a widespread phenomenon. Admittedly, numerous historical records mention the existence of relatively large towns in ancient civilizations, but such cities were organised mainly according to strict hierarchical political (if not military) principles in both spatial and social terms. As these cities owed their growth principally to administrative centralization, they often declined in importance when the central power of political regimes collapsed.

Urbanization in Europe since 1300 was initially based purely on gains from trade. Although some mechanization took place (for instance windmills), most towns still remained rather small (less than 20,000 inhabitants). Only when economic power was combined with administrative power (or a very strong accumulation of economic power only), did towns appear to exceed this limit. The industrial revolution in the last century changed this situation radically. The enormous economies of scale that could be achieved compared with the previous rural society, as well as the introduction of motive power and energy in urban and interurban transport, encouraged for the emergence of large cities. Therefore it is feasible to claim that modern urbanization is almost literally fuelled by the large scale introduction of fossil fuels. This also suggests that the transition of developing countries to a higher stage of development may cause a massive rise in energy consumption. This theory is reflected in the figures shown in Table 18.1.

Assuming that Germany is representative of a modern developed country in Europe, Table 18.1 also indicates that 'urban life' – in terms of availability of various energy sources and appropriate technical facilities – is a ubiquitous feature in Western Europe. It is also interesting to note a recent (modest) population decrease in various large cities (over 0.5 million inhabitants) in Western Europe, while many smaller and medium sized cities (50,000–150,000) appear to still be growing. On the other hand, in most Southern European countries urbanization is definitely an ongoing phenomenon. Here too, smaller cities grow, but the larger cities grow even faster. Athens, Barcelona or Madrid are notable examples of this rapid development. Consequently, the urbanization in the Southern member states of the European Community may induce an increase in the national (per capita) energy consumption in the countries concerned. The relationship between urbanization and energy consumption will be discussed later on in this chapter, with special reference to the cities participating in the CITIES programme.

Table 18.1 Energy densities in a developed and a developing country

	Germany	India
consumption per capita (kW):		
average	5	0.6
urban	5	2.0
rural	5	0.3

Source: Sassin (1982)

Although since the beginning of the 1970s the need for an efficient use of energy has shown various waves of acute interest (at least from the viewpoint of availability of energy resources), energy efficiency remains an important objective from an environmental viewpoint. Moreover, as long as fossil fuels dominate the energy mix, their limited availability should not be overlooked, particularly in view of ever-rising extraction costs. In addition, the access to fossil fuels (and the political power involved) is not uniformly spread.

Finally, in a competitive European economy cost efficient production is of the utmost importance, so that energy consumption will remain a major concern in business economics.

As already mentioned, towns are by definition centres of economic activity. Given that a concentration of activities implies a concentration of energy use, urban agglomerations, next to the international, national and regional level, seem to be a suitable geographical entity on which to focus on energy policy. Admittedly, large energy consuming industries have usually relocated from city centres to the urban fringe, but that leaves the impression of cities or urban agglomerations as large spatial concentrations of (direct and indirect) energy users which are essentially unaffected.

Energy policy objectives may – at least partly – be achieved by means of national measures, for instance the implementation of new technologies or the manipulation of prices. The improvement of energy efficiency being stimulated by a rise in energy costs in such an example. Also the introduction of new major energy sources, such as nuclear energy, is usually a national policy item. However, both the residential sector and small- and medium-sized firms need more stimuli than just price incentives to ensure that they are actually participating in energy efficiency actions. Demonstrations of the technical feasibility, information, consultancy and individual advice are usually the non-price ingredients for energy policy schemes in a decentralized setting. To ensure a sufficient impact, such facilities should be easily accessible for the target groups. In practice, this often means that their implementation must be realized at a decentralized (regional or local) level. Next, environmental policy – in comparison to energy policy – has to rely strongly on non-price measures, such as national – or preferably international – standards. Regarding the motivation of target groups environmental policy has to take into consideration the local environmental, social and economic situations. Furthermore, this decentralization argument has an important function in a bottom-up policy strategy, as it will usually require less effort to motivate and mobilize local inhabitants and interest groups for energy conservation and environmental programmes on a local or regional scale. Clearly the decentralization argument is in line with the current policy trend towards devolution.

In summary, the following points support the establishment of and policy support for urban energy policy schemes as advocated in the CITIES initiative:

• the city is a centre of economic activity and consequently a concentration of energy supply and energy consumption;
• local authorities have more insight and capabilities to shape urban energy policy in a way that is custom-made to the local situation;
• the establishment of local energy policies facilitates the involvement of local population, so that motivation and public support is easier to acquire;
• the municipality is often a more suitable geographical entity as regards data collection, statistical analysis and political competence.

ENERGY CONSUMPTION IN TWELVE EUROPEAN CITIES

The twelve cities in the **CITIES** programme exhibit a wide range of features. The population of the participating cities varies from just 25,000 (Esch/ Alzette) to more than 1 million (Torino). Some municipalities cover more or less the entire metropolitan area, such as Gent, Odense and Besançon. Others, however, are a dominant part of a larger conurbation, as in the case of Torino, Thessaloniki, Mannheim and Amsterdam. This feature may be important in the interpretation of energy statistics, such as consumption per capita. Yet in most cases the statistical information presented in this section applies exclusively to the participating municipalities. It should be noted that for Thessaloniki and Dublin all statistics apply to the agglomeration and for Newcastle part of the information applies to the region (see Table 18.2). The economic structure of the various cities also differs substantially. For instance, Torino and Mannheim have large industrial sectors, whereas Amsterdam is extremely service-oriented. An overview of economic key data is provided in Table 18.2.

Promotion of energy efficiency has been pursued for more than a decade in all member countries of the Community. Over the last ten years most countries have achieved some de-intensification of their economies (see Figure 18.1).

Table 18.2 Economic key data of twelve participating cities

city name	population (x 1000)	area (km²)	industry & building	services commercial	other
			economic structure (% of labour force)		
Amsterdam	720	126	19	52	29
Besançon	120	65	23	34	43
Bragança	100				
Cadiz	150	11	25	75	
Dublin*	910	300			
Esch/Alzette	25	15	57	43	
Gent	231	156	33	31	36
Mannheim	300	145	49	19	32
Newcastle**	286	103	31	3	37
Odense	175	102	32	35	33
Thessaloniki	706	137	37	63	
Torino*	1002	100	41	30	29

Note: * figures apply to agglomeration
   ** labour data apply to region

In Figure 18.1, four histograms are depicted for each member country. The two right hand histograms of each set of four represent the energy intensity of the economy in 1980 and 1987, respectively. The energy intensity in terms of the embodied energy per unit of GDP (here measured in Giga Joule per 1000 ECU (KECU)) decreased in most member countries, with the exception of Portugal, Greece and Ireland. Not surprisingly, these countries are exactly those that are still in the phase of classical urbanization (ie including strong industrialization), as discussed earlier.

Another energy efficiency measure is depicted by the first two (left hand) histograms of each set of four. These represent the ratio of final energy consumption to gross domestic energy consumption in 1980 and 1988 respectively. The ratio may be interpreted as the overall supply system efficiency for a given level (and composition) of final demand. The closer the ratio comes to one, the more efficient the supply system is likely to be. Here the general picture is less positive. Most countries report a decrease in overall energy systems efficiency. Notable exceptions are Luxembourg, Ireland and the United Kingdom, while the ratio remains constant in Germany.

A comparison of the two sets of histograms suggests a reverse relationship between the two indicators displayed in Figure 18.1. Theoretically, it is correct that a decrease of overall system efficiency (corresponding to a decrease in the left hand histograms) is correlated with an increase of energy intensity of the economy (corresponding with an increase in the right hand histograms). However, for various countries a high energy intensity of the economy coincides with a comparatively reasonable overall system

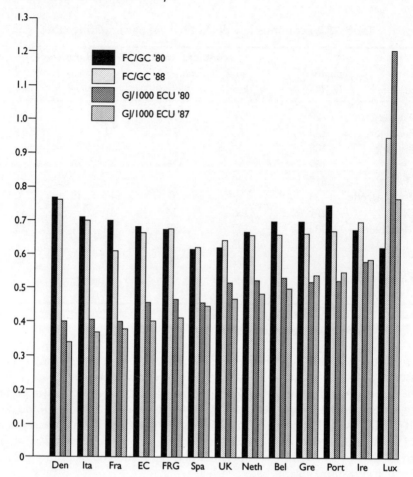

* 1987 is the last year for which complete statistics concerning GDP are currently available.

Source: Eurostat; participating cities

Figure 18.1 The development of energy efficiency indicators in the Community

efficiency. On the one hand, in the case of Belgium and the Netherlands this may be attributed to energy intensive activities using energy sources as primary energy, which is not regarded as final demand. On the other hand, in some countries the energy intensity of the economy is high due mainly to relatively low GDP levels, while industrialization has begun only recently. Consequently the intermediate use of energy (for chemicals or electricity generation) is relatively limited. Allowing for the primary energy effect in the low countries and the development effect in Greece, Portugal and Ireland, the importance of an efficient energy system is evident. Clearly, the less energy is needed for obtaining a certain amount of useful energy, the less energy intensive, *ceteris paribus*, the economy will be. We have to stress the – perhaps obvious – point that the causal relation runs from systems efficiency to energy intensity. The reverse is not necessarily true. A low energy intensity of an economy does not imply that an energy system is very efficient.

The information contained in Figure 18.1 reveals that Portugal and Greece are the only two countries experiencing both a decrease of the overall energy systems efficiency and an increased energy intensity in their economies. In other words, these countries not only used more energy for the transformation of primary resources, but they also needed more energy to keep their economy going (as a result of industrialization, motorization and so on). However, the original energy systems efficiency levels in these countries were rather high because of lower intermediate use of energy. Most probably, the combination of a decrease in overall systems efficiency and an increased energy intensity is related to ongoing urbanization fuelled by industrialization, motorization and a rapid increased use of electricity in household appliances.

In general, the decline of the overall energy system efficiency in most member countries may be largely explained by a greater proportion of electricity in final energy demand. As most countries succeeded in augmenting the value of their industrial production (for example a reorientation towards service industries or electronic engineering), the embodied energy per value unit of output decreased.

Although most countries managed to decrease the energy intensity of their economies, significant differences in the level of energy intensity still remain. In 1987, Denmark reported the lowest intensity (little heavy industry), followed by France and Italy (favourable climate). The Benelux countries have rather energy intensive economies (chemical industries, blast furnaces). From an ecological point of view, in economic terms this information alone is not very helpful, as the impacts on the environment depend on a number of other factors, including:

- the kinds of energy used;
- the availability of abatement facilities; and
- the spatial concentration of the energy consumption.

In order to gain more insight into this phenomenon, Figures 18.2 and 18.3 compare the energy consumption per capita in the various EC member countries as well as some other participating cities.* Denmark, for example, has a less advanced position per capita, while for instance France seems better off, especially if one takes into account that the population density in France is relatively low compared to most other Western European countries. The key factor, therefore, is that the prevailing climate and the

---

* Total Final Energy Consumption at the city level could not be obtained for all cities. Energy consumption of transport is particularly difficult to assess at this level. In general, energy statistics concerning the urban level are particularly reliable for network-provided energy carriers.

level of industrialization largely determine the energy consumption levels per capita in different countries.

The different stages of urbanization among European countries are also reflected in remarkable differences between urban and national consumption levels, as depicted in Figures 18.2 and 18.3. Notice that in Bresançon

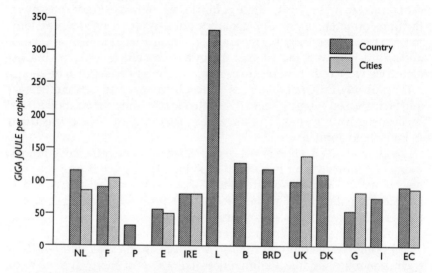

Figure 18.2 Final energy consumption per capita in EC countries and participating cities

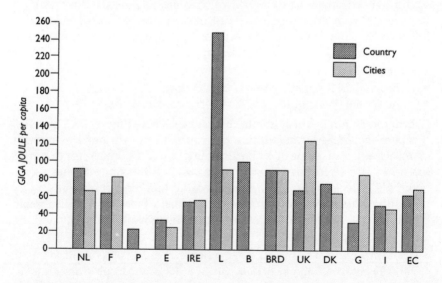

Figure 18.3 Final energy consumption per capita excluding transport in EC Countries and participating cities

and Thessaloniki the per capita consumption levels are above national levels, while in Amsterdam the opposite is true. Clearly this may be explained largely by the different economic bases of the cities concerned. Yet Torino – an industrial city – illustrates that such generalizations should be interpreted cautiously (Figure 18.3).

Finally, Figure 18.4. illustrates the per capita levels of electricity consumption for the twelve cities and their related countries.*

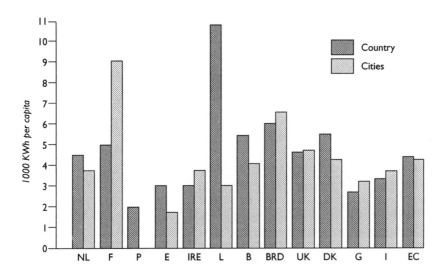

Figure 18.4 Final electricity consumption per capita in EC countries and participating cities

Compared to Figure 18.3, Mannheim and Torino are more energy intensive than the national average. The very high electricity consumption of Besançon is remarkable, and is probably because of the popularity of electric heating. To a lesser extent, electric heating perhaps also explains the shifts of Mannheim and Torino compared to Figure 18.3.

Most cities have implemented air quality measurement systems to enable monitoring on a regular basis. Those cities excluded from Figure 18.5 does not necessarily mean that no measurement system exists in that city. The figures represent crude annual averages for the entire city area,

---

* Electricity consumption per capita is here defined as the total urban consumption (industry, services and households) divided by the population size.

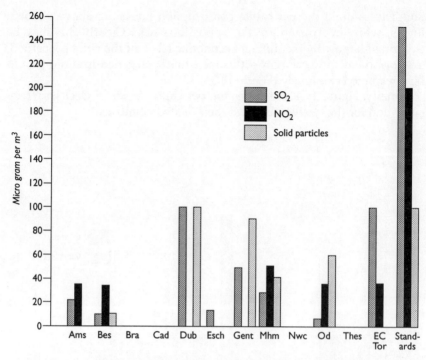

Figure 18.5 Air pollution indicators for some participating cities

yet seasonal and local variations may be quite large. For instance, even in apparently cleaner cities the air quality in narrow streets with heavy traffic may be unacceptable to residents. Moreover, the concentration of industry, particularly heavy industry, varies from negligible to very significant. For instance, cities with large chemical complexes in their vicinity have greater difficulty in achieving low pollution levels. Despite its limited value, Figure 18.5 does demonstrate that cities using mainly cleaner fuels such as natural gas enjoy on average a better air quality. Furthermore it shows that solid particles in the atmosphere are present in unacceptably high quantities.

19

European Cities and Sustainability Policy

MAIN ISSUES IN URBAN ENERGY POLICY

Closer analysis of the information provided by the cities involved in the **CITIES** project has led to the conclusion that the following policy areas largely make up the urban energy–environmental policy 'space':

- urban energy supply systems (UESS);
- urban waste management (UWM);
- urban transport systems (UTS);
- information, communication and marketing (ICM);
- management of the municipal building and vehicle stock (MBVS);
- development of integrative urban energy-environmental concepts (IUEC).

The twelve cities participating in the **CITIES** programme were not expected to report extensively on all these fields, but to select a few of most interest to them. Table 19.1 shows the choice of energy–environmental policy areas made by each of the participating cities. The empty entries in the table by no means imply that a city is not active. Clearly, one policy area may cover more than one project in a city, while some projects are related to several policy areas.

Energy management of the municipal capital stock is common practice in all participating cities. It may be regarded as the lower threshold level of a local energy policy. Clearly, a municipality should at least be capable of improving the efficiency of its own buildings and equipment. Usually this serves two objectives. First, it reduces the operating costs of the municipal capital stock and second, it serves as a good example to local firms and citizens.

The upper limit for local energy policy is an effective local management of energy supply systems. In the case of local management, the municipality (or its energy subsidiaries) has the opportunity to shape the system in a way that is optimal in terms of local environment, efficiency and reliability. Clearly it should be acknowledged that sometimes the surplus revenues of local energy companies are used for non-energy purposes (for example to cover financial deficits in municipal budgets), although such information is not given in the reports of participating cities.

Table 19.1 An overview of programmes and projects discussed in the city reports per policy area

	UESS*	UWM	UTS	ICM	MBVS	IUEC
Amsterdam	*			*		
Besançon			*		*	
Bragança	*					
Cadiz	*					
Esch-sur-Alzette	*				*	
Gent	*	*			*	
Dublin	*					
Mannheim	*					*
Newcastle		*		*	*	
Odense	*			*		
Thessaloniki		*	*			*
Torino	*					

Key:
UESS   urban energy supply systems
UWM   urban waste management
UTS   urban transport systems
ICM   information, communication and marketing
MBVS   management of municipal buildings and vehicle stock
IUEC   integrative urban energy concepts

In countries with strongly centralized (ie nationalized) energy supply companies, cities often have limited influence on the local supply system. Consequently the municipality has to focus its energy policy on other areas where it is more likely to make a significant impact. On the one hand, the municipality may decide to create local energy consultancy agencies aimed at supporting small commercial and residential energy consumers, which to a large extent circumvents the monopolistic power of national energy companies. On the other hand, in cases where the municipality chooses *not* to challenge the other major players, can choose to deal with issues that have another type of impact on energy consumption and the environment, such as urban transport systems. These appear to be a popular alternative to local energy policy, although interesting and promising results are only rarely found. Nevertheless, an efficient urban transport policy is undoubtedly worthy of research, as the transport sector is an important energy consumer in urban areas (approximately 25 per cent). Moreover, the environmental consequences are substantial in terms of both pollution and space. Generally, the energy and environmental aspects of urban transport policies result in a number of positive factors:

- the stimulation of public transport;
- the exclusion of private cars from some inner city areas;
- the creation of 'park and ride' facilities near main gateways to the city;
- encouraging people to use clean engines (preferably electric); and
- demonstration projects concerning the introduction of environmentally favourable (mainly public or semi-public transport) vehicles.

INSTITUTIONAL FRAMEWORK FOR URBAN SUSTAINABILITY POLICY

As indicated above, the institutional framework in a country determines to a large extent the maximum 'policy space' available for an urban energy and environmental policy. Based on the information from the twelve city reports, we have identified two criteria to describe the institutional framework for energy policy. The first criterion is the degree of centralization. The second is ownership status. The concept is illustrated in Figures 19.1 and 19.2. The vertical axis represents the degree of centralization. The top (C) indicates total centralization, while the bottom (D) denotes complete decentralization (municipality). The horizontal axis represents ownership status. 'Pu' at the extreme left indicates a real public enterprise (department), while 'Pr' denotes an entirely privately owned company. An intermediate situation is, for instance, a joint-venture (public-private partnership) or a limited company of which the majority of shares is owned by the state. The institutional 'types' may differ from system to system, but within any one system (gas, electric power) usually one type prevails. However, mixed situations may also exist, for instance when production transmission is primarily nationally managed, with distribution mainly locally managed. Moreover, some energy supply systems, such as the high-voltage electric power transportation grid, are always national, but the degree of local influence varies from country to country. The prevailing situations in some selected member states are depicted in Figures 19.1 and 19.2. However, in the United Kingdom the smaller but still important nationwide producer is privately owned, while the larger producer is still in public hands. This may well change in the near future, thus creating a mainly privatized electricity supply industry, therefore a dotted line in Figure 19.2 connects the two positions in the UK. Similarly in Italy local (distribution) companies own considerable amounts of power next to the national power system. A comparable situation may emerge in the Netherlands, if distribution companies continue to use their right to establish small scale power (less than 20 mw).

Undoubtedly, privatization is developing most quickly in the UK. The regional electricity companies in, for instance, Germany, Belgium and the Netherlands also have – in varying degrees – private sector characteristics. Here regional and local authorities ensure their influence by complete or partial ownership of the shares. There is, however, an important difference between the management of the entirely privatized energy companies in

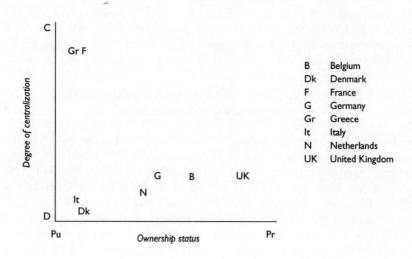

Figure 19.1 Institutional classification box – electricity distribution

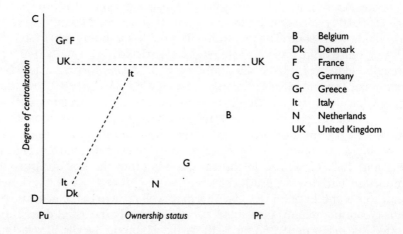

Figure 19.2 Institutional classification box – electricity production

the UK and the limited companies in Germany, the Netherlands and Belgium. The latter companies will usually be able to attract external capital by paying normal, or even reduced, long-term market interest rates. In the UK the energy companies have to compete fiercely with other investment alternatives, which implies current real rates of return of about 15 per cent. Consequently, British energy companies are very reluctant to invest yet they have to be very keen on a high utilization level of their capital stock.

Under certain conditions such incentives may frustrate energy conservation strategies. For instance, so-called 'valley filling' for electricity companies may be an attractive option. Where this is achieved by attracting new demand instead of shifting demand – and especially in case of substituting natural gas or district heating – this practice is incompatible with long-term energy efficiency programmes.

The state of the local economy is of course another important restriction on the actual possibilities of carrying out local energy programmes. Even if the 'policy space' is in principle available, other local problems may be perceived as more important by the municipality. For instance, several large cities suffering from urban and concomitant social decay prefer to focus their efforts on the improvement of the social and economic situation of the population in those parts of the city concerned. These efforts may include energy measures such as insulation in order to cut heating costs. Remarkably enough, the same kind of priority options may arise in economically extremely successful cities. Usually, the growth of the metropolitan area induced by economic thrift absorbs most of the municipalities' attention. Moreover, many municipalities do not dare to risk (as they see it) any decline in urban growth as a consequence of new measures aimed at the improvement of the energy efficiency and/or the environment.

PRINCIPAL RESULTS IN URBAN ENERGY–ENVIRONMENTAL POLICY

Urban energy supply systems

Referring to the overview of programmes and projects discussed in the above-mentioned city experiences, the following cities have paid particular attention to urban energy supply systems (UESS): Amsterdam, Bragança, Cadiz, Esch, Dublin, Gent, Mannheim, Odense and Torino. However, the discussion of the topics of this section will not be restricted to these towns only. UESS in regard to the energy policies chosen is analysed for all twelve cities participating in the study.

The possibilities for action and the degrees of freedom for the cities within the fields of UESS appear to depend on different conditions:

- institutional frameworks for energy planning activities and energy policies (energy planning, environmental planning or urban planning);
- supplier systems organization and ownership, and related decision structures;
- financial possibilities or constraints;
- energy pricing and competition between different energy sources;
- socio–cultural environment and traditions for UESS.

The analysis of the UESS, often narrowly defined as, for instance, electricity, steam and domestic heat, natural gas, and solid and liquid fuel supply, comprises also other energy measures proposed or carried out within the fields of energy savings as well as transportation. The only UESS common to all cities is the electricity distribution grid, which is operated and managed by national, regional or municipal companies.

The electricity supply is presently considered as reliable. However, the increase of load demands leads – in addition to the construction of new capacity – to different kinds of saving measures ranging from the promotion of low energy lighting (Amsterdam, Odense, Besançon) and the improvement of low voltage network and public lighting (Torino) to more financially-oriented measures such as encouraging reduction of expensive power purchases during high tariff periods by help of local diesel generation (Besançon, Esch) or by introducing load-differentiated tariffs to reduce the demand during the peak load period (Thessaloniki and Gent, especially for electric heating).

It appears that the largest improvements in power distribution and consumption are realized by cities with a municipality-owned electricity company (Torino and Amsterdam). In the other cases the electricity savings are limited to the municipal buildings and services. The municipal ownership of power plants seems to be a determining factor for the promotion of CHP (combined heat and power) concepts and large DH (district heating) systems (for example the case of Torino with the implementation of new CHP plants and the conversion of an existing thermal plant into CHP). This consideration applies also to Gent and Mannheim, although in Mannheim an important part of the DH is now provided through a transmission system from a regional power company.

In other cases, financial advantages obtained by CHP and competitiveness of combined production compared to other available energy sources are the main arguments for the development. The fact that 90 per cent of domestic heating demand in Odense is covered by the cheapest DH delivery in Denmark based on CHP from a regional power company confirms this point of view. In the cases of Amsterdam and Newcastle, recent changes in prices for natural gas following the fluctuations of the oil market in Holland and England reinforce the financial reliability of small and medium gas fired CHP units.

In addition to ownership, the existence of a planning framework seems to play an important role in the development of UESS. In three cities (Torino, Mannheim and Odense) where a comprehensive energy planning has been carried out, the physical, institutional and operational allocation of competence, responsibilities and restrictions has led to successful and complementary implementation and development of several UESS. This includes DH, gas networks, restrictions concerning individual heating systems and improved energy saving measures.

For the other cities where energy planning does not have the same favourable conditions, measures taken in the field of UESS are weaker or largely absent. The difficulties of the Dublin Gas Company and the absence of a DH system in Amsterdam, where planning failed because of lack of competence and incentives for the private sector, are two examples. In some cases, it is environmental concern and planning which induce new energy measures (energy management and savings as well as transportation planning).

Finally, other socio–cultural factors should not be neglected in considering the role and place of UESS in the various cities. For example, the low percentage of central heating systems in Dublin and the traditional use of solid fuel (bituminous coal and peat) are some of the socio–cultural constraints to expansion of the natural gas supply. On the other hand, immediate prosperous socio–cultural opportunities (such as the very high share of municipal and private rental housing in Amsterdam) did not contribute to the development of UESS such as district heating.

There is no one recipe for the successful development of UESS. However, the cities with well developed UESS in the case studies have some figures and conditions in common which seem to be favourable for a successful application of UESS:

- Existence of a legal background to initiate an organization dealing with planning and construction activities in the energy sector.
- Participation of all competitive energy supply systems in planning activities (as members or associates of the energy organization).
- Financial capacity of the organization in charge of the implementation of the energy planning (such as public or semi-public funding).
- Partial control of tariff policies applied to the consumers.
- Follow-up procedures to ensure successful implementation of UESS (information campaigns, subsidies, etc).

Urban waste management

Among the many new environmental challenges facing public policymakers, waste treatment is usually a municipal responsibility. Urban waste management may take two forms:

1. *Processes which do not produce directly usable energy*
   The practice of dumping waste in landfills takes up a lot of space and is harmful to the environment (even in the case of controlled dumping). In contrast, biological recycling of waste (for example composting) transforms waste by biological fermentation. After crushing and sifting household waste, biologically nondegradable materials are eliminated; the remaining waste is then exposed to fermentation processes. Such processes can be slow (two or three months) or accelerated (four to fourteen days). A final refining stage adapts the product to user needs. The result is a compost which raises the organic matter content and may be used for many purposes, such as fertilizer for agricultural land.
2. *Processes which directly produce energy*
   For (solid) households waste the following options can be

distinguished:

- **Recycling:** Glass, paper, plastics and metal can be recycled, thereby generating energy savings in the fabrication of these materials. Such materials can also be sold to the industry, as they may be very useful as raw materials.
- **Incineration** with heat recovery (solid wastes): The energy contained in urban waste can be recovered by producing steam for heat (a district heating network, for example) or electricity (auto-producer or industrial use). This significantly lowers the overall costs of treatment and elimination of urban wastes, and is a very suitable treatment for large cities, where waste quantities are enormous, landfill space limited and energy needs are more concentrated. It does require, however, large investments, therefore this technique is only appropriate for urban areas of at least 100,000 inhabitants, making up a waste resource of 35,000 metric tons per year or 100 metric tons per day (ie four to five tons per hour).
- **Methane production:** With methane production, it is possible to extract the energy from the fermentable household waste (biogas is principally methane) and burnable component of digestible organic matter. Agricultural applications are also possible. Many processes are currently being implemented in Europe, for example in France. Here the process VALORGA contains:
  - *initial crushing by conventional means;*
  - *simplified sorting (sifting and iron and steel removal);*
  - *kneading or watering of waste material;*
  - *15 day storage period in a digester for the production of biogas and a digestate;*
  - *compacting in order to reduce humidity in the digestate and prepare it for sale;*
  - *sorting out inert solids with high energy contents.*

Methane production from sewage waste has primarily been developed in large urban sewage treatment plants (more than 100,000 inhabitants). The production of biogas for energy use by methanization of residual sludge is feasible in sewage treatment plants that have a circuit of anaerobic stabilization of sludge by digestion. When kept at approximately 35°C in the absence of air, a biological reaction occurs in the sewage sludge with biogas production (60 to 70 per cent CH_4, 30 to 40 per cent CO_2). Some of this gas is burnt in a boiler to preheat the sludge before it enters the digester, and to maintain the temperature of the latter. About 65 per cent of the biogas remains: it can be used to heat nearby buildings or to produce electricity with a generator (cogeneration).

Urban transport systems

In recent years the European transport scene has shown drastic changes. Mobility has increased and at the same time congestion has increased in almost all transport modes. It is also increasingly recognized that transport plays a vital role in building up an integrated European network economy. At the same time there is growing awareness of the high (sometimes unacceptable) social costs of transport (notably in the area of land use and the environment). Transport has recently become a focal point of research and policy interest because of the conflicting roles it plays in our modern society.

It is interesting to observe that in most European countries there is also a strong decentralization tendency in transport policy, sometimes even accompanied by privatization. Such devolution of transport policy was not only induced by the weak financial or budget situation of public agencies in charge of transport, but was also favoured by worldwide changes in the transportation sector. In the past decade European transport has undergone a wide variety of – sometimes problematic – developments at both local/regional and national/international levels. Despite the increasing popularity of Just-in-Time (JIT) systems and related concepts, the actual practice of both commodity and passenger transport is disappointing and often frustrating. Severe traffic congestion phenomena at the urban or metropolitan level (for instance in Athens, Rome, Paris), unacceptable delays in medium- and long-distance transport during peak hours, unsatisfactory service levels of most public transport systems etc. It is even claimed increasingly that a free European market may lead to unacceptable accessibility conditions in major regions in Europe.

As a result of many divergences, nowadays transport policymakers in most European countries and cities find themselves in extremely complicated situations. A large number of interest groups, ranging from multinational companies to local environmentalists, urges them to take action. Often, however, this pressure to act pulls in quite different directions. On the one hand, it has become obvious that the environment poses its limits on the volume, character and pace of the extension of the transport infrastructure. On the other hand, most firms in Western Europe are concerned about their competitiveness in a global context due to an inadequate infrastructure.

It turns out that in recent years environmental impediments have become critical in the evaluation of new transport systems and of current mobility patterns at the urban level. For example, air quality improvement is one of the motivations behind the public transport priority plan in Besançon. The overall main problem in environmental policy is that environmental decay is not easy to capture in conventional economic-financial calculation schemes. The allocation of scarce resources will – in the view of a conventional economist – lead to an equilibrium between desire and possibility (or between supply and demand) via the intermediate tool of the market mechanism. This mechanism is giving price signals as a way of generating adequate responses of economic players. The system however, only works properly if all costs and revenues are reflected in the price mechanism. Failure to do so leads to biased signals and hence to inappropriate behaviour. For instance, if noise annoyance of cars is not adequately imputed to the source, an overuse of cars will take place. This shortcoming in the price system is often termed market failure.

There is, however, also a related problem which may sometimes even intensify the impacts of such market failures. In many countries and cities, the existence of market failures has led to government responses in order to restore the balance. This is only successful if the measures imposed ensure that all social costs are fully reflected in the price signals of a market system. Such measures may be financial in nature (for example charges, subsidies or taxes), but may also include non-financial methods (regulations, standards or prohibitions). In all cases, the effects of such measures should be such that they charge economic players with all marginal social costs, either directly or indirectly. If this is not done, an efficient market equilibrium will not be reached, or in the worst case the government response may even lead to a further deviation from a social optimum. Such intervention failures may arise because public decisionmakers are often unable to interpret biased signals properly. And indeed in many countries and cities we have witnessed the existence of response failures of the government.

Two examples may clarify this case. Parking policy in the Dutch city of Utrecht has aimed at reducing car use by restricting the number of parking places, but as a result most car drivers were driving further (and hence causing more air pollution) in order to find a parking place. Traffic restraint policy in Athens has tried to reduce car use by introducing the system of even and odd number plates for entering the inner city circle on a given day, but as a result car drivers were travelling much further in order to get as close as possible to the circular ring around the city (thus causing even more traffic annoyance).

It is thus clear that public intervention in urban transport is a risky matter, as people will always find ways of circumnavigating intervention measures. Given the rigidity in government behaviour, in various countries and cities severe intervention failures seemed to emerge. The transport sector is a glaring example of the existence of a great many of such response failures.

Clearly there are also examples of response successes. The introduction of rapid railway systems in Europe and the recent improvement of the level of service of some public transport means signs of success may be seen in various European countries in which mobility and transport are brought in harmony with another. In general, however, urban transport policies in European cities are not very well developed and not very strongly oriented toward energy saving and environmental preservation. In the set of urban case studies only two examples can be identified with an explicit focus on energy conservation: Besançon and Thessaloniki.

Besançon has implemented a traffic circulation plan aiming to discourage through traffic in the city, to give priority to collective transport and to allow space for pedestrian zones. Especially for collective transport, ambitious success rates have been set (95 per cent coverage of urban population within a radius of 300 metres from a boarding place). The use of collective forms of transport is far higher than in comparable French cities. This leads to considerable energy savings, as for instance a bus consumes five times less energy per passenger kilometre than a private car. The present policy aims to improve the level of service and the penetration of collective transport in suburban areas.

Thessaloniki has also made several attempts at improving the traffic situation by creating ring roads, a better system of public transport and the construction of a light metro system. As transport consumes 25 per cent of urban final energy consumption, considerable gains are to be expected, as well as environmental benefits. For instance, a light metro system consumes only approximately 33 per cent of fuel use per passenger compared to buses. Also other facilities such as special bus lanes are being considered. The expected social benefits may have a great deal of public support. Moreover, traffic plans are embedded in an overall City Master Plan for Thessaloniki, thereby introducing comprehensive planning in the city.

The general conclusion is that urban transport systems policy with a clear environmental and energy focus is lacking in most cities. Apart from the design of advanced hardware and software components of such systems, critical success factors are:

- environmental compatibility;
- sound financing schemes; and
- efficient organizational and institutional structures for designing and managing such systems.

Information, communication and marketing

Apparently most cities have employed marketing and information techniques in order to promote and carry out their energy policies. As already indicated, special emphasis on information, communications and marketing has been given by three cities participating in the CITIES programme: Odense, Amsterdam and Newcastle upon Tyne. It should be pointed out that the experience drawn by these cities is not to be conceived as a panacea for a successful replication of energy saving measures in all other cities: it should serve only as an insight to the possibilities offered to planners and decisionmakers, by correct adaptation of information, communication and marketing strategies to the special characteristics of the targeted social groups.

In 1979, the city of Odense started a process of restricted energy management in public buildings. Part of this programme concerned the information and training of responsible persons and users of public buildings, especially as far as the implementation of energy saving measures is concerned. An important part of the whole project concerned the appointment of an 'energy officer' for each public building. The energy officers were given the responsibility for all energy matters, and supported in technical and economic matters by the municipal energy consultant. According to energy department estimations, during the period 1981–1988 the total of energy saving investments (including the information and training programme) had reached the amount of 6.5 million ECU, while the total energy saved as a result of implementation of the programme has exceeded 8.9 million ECU.

The city of Amsterdam has promoted the use of energy saving lamps in the city's domestic sector. The aim was twofold: energy saving lamps would reduce the overall electricity demand of the city, thus considerably reducing energy costs for the inhabitants; and the substitution of such bulbs for conventional incandescent lamps would allow for substantial reduction of the electricity production capacity, which otherwise would have to be compensated by imported energy during peak demand hours. In order to promote this scheme, the Energy Company Amsterdam motivated the producers of energy saving lamps and the retail sector of the city to cooperate and to provide incentives to their potential customers in order to render the product more attractive during the initial period of the programme. As a result of the lower prices offered to the public, of the direct approach of the Energy Company to the public, and by partially financing customers for the purchase of two to four lamps, the project has been considered a success, as it is expected to result in an annual reduction of electricity consumption of about 11 Gwh.

Households account for up to 36 per cent of the total primary energy consumption of Amsterdam. Consequently, the city's Energy Company directed a lot of its action on energy saving through interventions in the city's domestic sector. A so-called E-team was formed. Their task was to provide information and elementary repair work to tenants complaining about high energy bills. The E-team aims at an improvement of energy efficiency in old houses through low costs schemes. The Energy Company has publicized the team in various languages spoken in the city and in the form of cartoon-like publications.

In the city of Newcastle upon Tyne, Council policy is implemented through a highly organized Energy Management and Informations Unit that provides services to energy consumers within the region. The Unit provides services in both technological aspects and on giving promotion, advice and information. The Unit directs most of its information services towards the domestic consumer, although some information is also provided for small businesses and school projects. More specifically, the Unit provides advice to the housing sector, in the form of tenants information leaflets that are supplied to council tenants when a new heating system is installed. In addition, the Unit acts as a liaison between the fuel boards and individuals who are to be disconnected from the fuel supply or who have difficulty paying their bills. Moreover, it acts as the administrative centre for the Fuel Liaison Group, which is a forum for the discussion on domestic fuel supply issues.

An important activity of the Unit is the provision of general information on insulation, heating and ventilation. This is done through exhibitions, publication of leaflets, and in-house training courses in Energy Awareness. The Unit also provides information and promotes energy saving activities in Industry and Commerce. This is achieved through a variety of measures, such as the Task Force. This comprises Energy Managers who work on a voluntary basis and provide recommendations for small businesses in the city. In parallel to this activity, the Unit provides general information on energy saving measures applicable to industry. The Unit is in contact with 'Keeping Newcastle Warm', the local heating advice and insulation project, which is part of the national charity Neighbourhood Energy Action. In the area of incentive schemes and good housekeeping, the Unit has set up the Environment 2000 Energy Leaders Scheme that encouraged children to switch off lights through a mass of different promotion activities; the scheme resulted in a spectacular saving of approximately ECU 20,000 over the first year for an initial publicity investment of ECU 6700.

Irrespective of the actual degree of success of the specific information campaigns and promotion measures, it should be noted that in most energy saving projects at the urban level, information, communication and marketing are of a fundamental importance, as the projects themselves require the active participation of city inhabitants. Since in most cities the domestic sector is the largest energy consumer, energy saving should achieved through action in this sector. City inhabitants should be well informed about their opportunities and responsibilities and should be attracted by targeted marketing techniques. It appears, though, that participation varies along with the overall social and economic development of the city, and even the people's norms and attitudes, as inhabitants base their participation in energy saving tasks in relation to their direct living priorities and necessities. In other words, one may expect that projects much dependent on citizen participation will be more successful in cities where social indicators are more advanced. In order to cope with such projects in developing cities, the techniques to be adopted should be designed on the basis of local characteristics, and in certain cases the energy saving character of the whole project should probably be downgraded in favour of other seemingly 'more important' properties of the project.

Management of the municipal building and vehicle stock

Each city usually owns an appreciable building stock and various public services have substantial vehicle fleets as well. In most cases the operational costs of municipal buildings and vehicles* have to be paid from the annual budget. Consequently, after the oil price rises, municipalities had (and still

---

* The vehicle fleet of public transport services is not included in this section, neither are municipal housing services. The municipal building stock consists typically of offices, schools and colleges, sports and leisure facilities, theatres and special buildings such as police and fire stations.

have) strong and clear interests in cutting energy costs of their buildings and vehicles. Therefore, virtually all cities may be expected to undertake at least some sort of energy management of their buildings and vehicles. Yet in our comparative EC review, four cities appeared to focus their efforts explicitly concerning energy management schemes on their own buildings and vehicles, namely Besançon, Gent, Newcastle and Odense. For this reason the following discussion below is based primarily on the information provided by these four cities, though other cities will be mentioned incidentally.

Apart from the obvious reason of reducing operating costs of building and vehicle stock, municipalities also operate energy management schemes that set an example for the local energy actions of the public in general. Sometimes such schemes may be used for testing new technical or organizational concepts (for instance, in Gent); finally they can be used as an information source for municipal energy consultancy agencies.

A relatively new argument affecting energy efficiency programmes in general – but definitely energy management schemes relating to building stock – is the emergence of national and local environmental plans which include the issue of increasingly strict emission standards. Apart from purely efficiency-oriented schemes, often this implies fuel switching of heating equipment. Clearly, setting a good example plays a role in this respect. For instance, Besançon reports that by 1988, 90 per cent of its oil fired heating equipment was replaced by natural gas fired types. As well as being less polluting, the new installations turn out to be more efficient, thus allowing a pay-back time of two and a half years.

A crucial aspect of the municipal energy management schemes is sound and clear organization of information, production, collection, processing and retrieval. On the one hand this requires sufficient institutional backing in the entire municipal organization. Odense, Newcastle, Gent and Amsterdam witness municipal-wide organizations (Steering Committees, Energy Cells, etc), in which all major parties (aldermen, representatives of main departments, technical specialists, and so on) are represented.

On the other hand, the actual collection and treatment of energy and financial data should, as much as possible, be based on fixed arrangements. Not surprisingly, the impressive cost reductions and the new possibilities of telematics have greatly enhanced the large-scale introduction of computerized measurement in all cities concerned. The application of telematics allows the use of comprehensive data bases. These data bases can be used to compare actual performance data with relevant standards. Newcastle's report provides extensive examples of the use of performance indicators. Subsequently, numerical targets (at any desired level) may be formulated as a basis for action plans. Of course, the available information has to be used sensibly in feedback procedures *vis-à-vis* the various municipal departments. In the case of larger action plans involving substantial investments, special financial energy consultants (internal or external) are contacted to enable a proper assessment of the proposed investments.

As regards the fields of interest, space heating takes the most prominent place in all cities. Gent, Newcastle and Odense report special attention paid to typical large energy consumers such as swimming pools. In Gent, a reduction of natural gas consumption of 30 per cent is reported after the retrofit of the air conditioning and pool water equipment. Several cities mention the retrofit of lighting equipment. In particular, Besançon pays attention to the electricity costs, *inter alia* by applying load management through small-scale generation. This last option can be explained by the tariff structure of Electricité de France (EDF) involving various peak prices. The city of Esch recently installed a total energy installation to serve a complex of public buildings. The benefits of this system are based on the national use of energy as well as the facility to use the system to cover peak electricity demand.

The optimization of the energy efficiency of the vehicle fleet seems complicated. No single city witnesses explicit results in this area. Probably the efficiency improvements incorporated in new car models has mitigated the fuel bill, but this achievement can be attributed mainly to the vehicle manufacturers. Other measures, such as optimizing vehicle use, require rather advanced organizational tools (and new information) and as such this may impede their introduction in municipal organizations.

The overall performance of the energy management schemes for municipally owned building stock is very satisfactory. Besançon reports accumulated buildings efficiency investments of approximately 32 million FF. The accumulated energy savings represent a value of 21 million FF. In Odense accumulated energy investments presently reach a value of 51 million Dkr., while the accumulated value of savings is rated at 71 million Dkr. In 1988 the energy costs of the municipality of Besançon constituted 3.8 per cent (28 million FF) of the total budget. In the absence of energy saving measures the costs would have been 32 million FF.

Integrative urban energy–environmental concepts

Systems of energy supply to urban areas which guarantee that the following principles are simultaneously followed can be termed **integrative concepts**. These are as follows:

- Secure availability of choice among (at least two) sources of energy.
- Acceptability of energy production and transformation technologies from an environmental point of view.
- Cost-consciousness in production and distribution of energy.
- Priceworthy supply of energy sources to users.

In order to ensure energy availability it is necessary that supply equals (or exceeds) demand at any time, which means that either production can react flexibly to demand increases or reserve capacities can be tapped easily. This condition should hold good not only for electricity, but for at least one further centrally supplied energy source such as natural gas or/and district heating, in order to give the customers the necessary freedom of choice, and not to cause them to revert to the environmentally undesirable use of decentralized sources of heat or power (coal, oil etc). Obviously, under the aspects of pollution and noise emission control, designing and operating of an efficient public transport system is required as well as the installation of adequate technological devices in energy production facilities themselves.

Prerequisites for cost- and price-consciousness from the view of the energy supplier are, on the one hand, adaptation of modern technology and efficient organizational structures and, on the other hand, devising an appropriate pricing system that caters to the needs of the various types of energy users in the short and in the long run. Prices should be sufficient to cover costs and to allow for the financing of future investments in order to secure long-term productivity, but no excess profits should be envisioned. Low-priced minimum supply arrangements for private households should be provided out of a sense of social responsibility; yet unnecessary consumption should be prohibited through differential pricing practice for reasons of energy conservation. Cost-appropriate prices for business use of energy are a necessary condition for securing competitiveness of the local and regional economy.

The principles mentioned are to be considered as policy objectives for the management of urban energy systems; however, flexibility should be provided for entrepreneurial initiatives and the ways of following them through. Thus, the discrepancy between policy direction and executive action should be well recognized in order not to hamper individual creativity in adapting policy to particular local conditions.

In fact, in all cities where Integrative Urban Energy Concepts today play a major role as guidance mechanisms for local energy supply, external incentives in the form of legal regulations or conditions for participation in public support programmes have given impetus for developing such concepts. Dublin, for example, explicitly mentions the incentive value of the 1980 EC Council Directive on air quality for the installation of an adequate atmospheric monitoring system and the identification of quality targets to be achieved in a pre-defined time scale. In the German National Energy Programme of 1973 and its extensions, the expansion of district heating systems has been explicitly named as an instrument, or a concrete objective of energy policy. In 1974, the Federal Ministry of Research commissioned a number of regional studies for district heating development, among others a study for the Mannheim region, where the first efforts to establish a district heating system date back to 1938/39. Based on the results of this study, in 1977 Stadtwerke Mannheim initiated its district heating demonstration project, supported by federal funds within the nationwide Programme for Investments in the Future. Today in Mannheim, 38.3 per cent of all residential units are served with district heating (another 37.4 per cent are heated by means of natural gas or electricity).

The designing, and in particular, the implementation of Integrative Urban Energy–Environmental Concepts will benefit from the existence of adequate organizational structures which may, however, differ in various cities due to the socio–political framework. In Mannheim, a structure has been set up which relies totally on a system of interrelated companies based on corporate law regulations. Mannheimer Versorgungs- und Verkehrs Gesellschaft mbH (Mannheim Utilities and Transport Ltd) as the holding is fully owned and controlled by the city. This company in turn owns and directs three corporations that deal with the various fields of utility production and procurement, supply and distribution to customers and public transport. This construction makes it possible to systematically encompass the various aspects in the concept as well as to react flexibly to the implementation procedure through entrepreneurial action.

In Odense, on the other hand, the utilities and the public transport are fully integrated as one department in the city administration. This organizational concept places more emphasis on the political decision making procedure, and gives more room for and higher priority to non-business socio–environmental objectives. In the Torino model, a high importance is attached to cooperation between city officials and scientific and technical advisors, in coordination with regional authorities and national energy institutions.

A final lesson to be drawn here is that, irrespective of the political question of which particular organizational provisions and institutions may be preferable under specific political, legal, and economic conditions, integrated energy strategies should be such that:

- transfer of new information;
- adaption of technological development;
- accessibility of investment capital; and
- coordination of the various segments of the system are facilitated as much as possible in the prevailing context of urban policies and citizens' participation.

CONCLUSION

The cross-Community review of urban energy projects has revealed that virtually every city in Europe recognizes the importance of local energy and environmental policy. Yet the policy space is very much influenced by the institutional organization of the energy systems and responsibilities concerning security of supply, price level, environmental standards and so on. These are usually a national matter and may be influenced depending on the degree of market functioning and the ownership and taxation of exhaustible resources, such as fossil fuels. Given any national energy policy framework, additional local and regional energy plans always seem necessary to offer a detailed implementation framework in addition to – often rather generally – formulated national policy goals (such as an overall efficiency improvement of 20 per cent).

As regards the institutional organization, scale economies may be a sensible indicator, as far as they are separately assessed for constituent parts of the system such as generation, distribution, etc. Separating generation (or main transport) from distribution may be accompanied by integrating the distribution of several network-provided energy carriers at the local level. In other words, vertical integration is, to some extent, substituted by horizontal integration. As regards ownership status, there is some tendency to various forms of private companies, although public influence remains decisive in most cases, except for the UK.

The various cases presented here underscore the importance of a comprehensive approach to urban energy–environmental projects. Though a concrete project may aim at a specific goal related to a particular aspect of the energy market, it always involves other items included in the list of most crucial issues presented above. For instance, information and communication including updating and feedback are vital aspects for any project.

The overall conclusion from this survey is that urban energy–environmental policy may be an effective strategy in the context of both economizing on energy costs and improving urban environmental quality. Consequently, the aim of a sustainable city requires intensive efforts for combined energy–environmental policy initiatives and operational strategies. The various experiences of European cities have brought to light interesting learning examples and also important caveats for implementing effective policies for urban sustainable development.

20

Sustainable Cities: Retrospect and Prospect

SPACE FOR URBAN SUSTAINABILITY INITIATIVES

Urban areas – notably agglomerations – are increasingly becoming focal points of policy and competition, not only inside the European Community but also outside. This has many important consequences for energy and environmental policy: urban areas form a 'natural' concentration point for efficient and effective energy and environmental policy initiatives. Interesting examples of urban sustainability initiatives can be found in the following areas:

- **Urban waste and energy efficiency.** In this area problems like pollution of urban areas, recycling of material, the potential of biogas, maintenance of energy systems (standards, evaluation) and so on play a critical role.
- **Transportation, energy and environment.** The vehicle stock in many cities is usually outdated (with high energy use and pollution emission), the infrastructure design has negative consequences for energy efficiency and the management and routing of traffic flows is usually not very well developed. In consequence, there is a serious gap between the actual and the potential performance of urban transport systems.
- **Built environment, energy and environment.** The stock of public and private buildings is usually not well maintained, and insulation measures are often neglected, leading to high energy consumption and noise annoyance, with the effect on human health and on urban monuments taking its toll.

Apart from these three major problem areas, in many countries the issue of public housing (for instance the juridical status in relation to the (in)ability to operate the housing stock efficiently), and of the ownership and management of energy networks (especially in relation to integration and separation of production and distribution), is also at stake. Thus severe energy and environmental problems at the urban level can be observed in many countries.

In developing strategies for improving this situation, it should be recognized that energy problems – and related environmental and health problems – are diverse among countries and cities. Various cities have managed to cope in a creative way with these problems, while others are still lagging behind. There is an apparent need for a better exchange of information on critical success factors that have enabled energy/ environmental policies in various countries to achieve a degree of success. There is no doubt that a significant improvement in urban energy/ environmental conditions in Eastern Europe, the Mediterranean and Third World cities is also possible.

In the light of the previous observations, it seems a sensible strategy to formulate and propose urban energy/environmental initiatives with the following statement of objectives: the promotion of an effective and efficient urban energy/environmental policy aiming at 1. a maximum feasible reduction in all forms of direct and indirect energy consumption in cities, and 2. a rational choice of urban environmental management procedures and techniques contributing to a further enhancement of the efficiency of urban energy systems and related environmental quality conditions.

Those goals are in harmony with the general policy objectives which focus on ecologically sustainable economic development, as formulated in the well-known Brundtland report on 'Our Common Future'.

The development of urban initiatives in the area of energy– environmental management presupposes that cities have sufficient political willingness and space to do so. This scope for action may vary from one city to another, and from one member state to another. A common element in all sustainability policies is that many technically possible solutions are not applied because of institutional problems of a legal and/or economic nature. Some principal obstacles which can be quoted in this context are the legal right of gas and electricity distribution reserved to the central power units, and monopoly situations of energy producers dominating the market with very marginal prices for feeding into the public grid electricity produced by individuals (factories, hospitals, waste incinerators, etc). A major task for the near future is to abolish these conflicts of interest between local, regional and national competences and jurisdictions in the area of energy supply and environmental policy. Institutional coordination has to be strongly encouraged as a strategy for ensuring the lowest social costs of a combined energy–environmental policy in cities. Such institutional cooperation has to be based on sound economic–financial principles and may also incorporate private initiatives and public–private partnership.

Another problem arises with the multiple players situation in urban environmental policy. In the case of large numbers of parties the implementation of an effective policy is fraught with many difficulties, urban transport being the best example. Nevertheless, urban governments have the competence and potential to reduce many of the negative externalities associated with urban transport.

In this concluding chapter we will reflect on the above-mentioned issues, namely, institutional bottlenecks, urban environmental management (notably waste treatment) and multiple-party problems (notably in transport). Also the importance of marketing and information provision to the public will be emphasized, while we conclude with a repeated plea for European urban sustainability policies.

INSTITUTIONAL BARRIERS

Various case studies from many countries point at the limited degree of flexibility in urban energy–environmental planning. This is caused by rigid institutional barriers or administrative competences reflecting a self-interest of some established interest groups. It should be added, however, that reluctance to accept decentralized energy options at a local scale is often strongly dependent on the lack of convincing arguments. Urban energy planning may be regarded broadly as an appropriate policy option when it is clearly demonstrated that it is technically feasible and economically meaningful.

Rational arguments – taking into consideration the market situation and the technology potential – may remove institutional obstacles for urban energy and environmental planning. Arguments to be used in this context include:

- financial funding for all parties;
- favourable environmental effects;
- more competitiveness in view of the open European market;
- contribution to deregulation (including public–private partnership);
- flexibility in terms of production and distribution of energy in adjusting to small-scale energy options;
- better matching of long- and short-term energy planning.

In general, an urban energy planning system of incentives based on efficient cooperation is always to be preferred to monopolization which is alienating and leads to inertia and bureaucracy.

WASTE TREATMENT

Urban waste management has proven to be an effective strategy for serving both environmental and energy purposes. Cities should be encouraged to intensify their efforts in this area, especially because urban waste treatment appears to be an economically viable policy which, at the same time, is able to eliminate high social and environmental costs. Very often, management of waste has been handled on a much broader scale than urban alone and has necessitated both local and regional coordination. Urban waste management should be based on three consecutive principles: avoidance of waste, recycling of waste material and incineration (rather than disposing) of waste. Waste treatment can be undertaken by both private and public enterprises, but in both cases the ultimate aim should be to generate social benefits out of urban waste.

TRANSPORT POLICY

Transport is an important energy consumer, claiming approximately 25 to 30 per cent of primary energy consumption by end use (mainly petroleum). Consequently the environmental impacts of transport are significant, and as the majority of people now live in urban areas, it is clear that transport and the quality of urban life are closely linked.

Many cities are worried about the high social costs of urban transport and many – often *ad hoc* – urban transport policies are being developed. A clear link with resource (energy and environmental) targets is often lacking. In this context it is noteworthy that the use of price mechanisms as an effective tool for coping with urban environmental externalities (such as urban road pricing, urban toll systems, etc) is never – or hardly – ever used. Furthermore, long-term strategies (for example settlement (re)distribution policy) in the context of an overall urban planning strategy is rare, but ought to be encouraged.

Urban transport management options refer mainly to short- and medium-term ways of influencing urban transport behaviour in order to ensure a more efficient transport system or to reduce environmental or other external costs (see Newman and Kenworthy 1991). Examples are:

- optimizing urban transport network flows (such as coordinated traffic lights, electronic route guidance systems etc);
- road pricing or user charge measures (for instance the Singapore model, or the recent experiences in Oslo or Stockholm);
- auto restraint measures (for example closing inner city areas, such as in Milan);
- car- or van-pooling and/or special lanes on motorways for car-poolers;
- information and communication campaigns;
- integration of fare systems in an urban area in order to enhance inter-system connections and thereby improving the accessibility and usefulness of public transport (for example the national 'strip-card' for public transport in the Netherlands).

In various cases a combination of such management options has to be chosen (Webster et al 1988; Wegener et al 1991). Urban transport strategies refer to medium- and long-term measures which have a structural impact on the mobility pattern in urban areas. Two types of measures may be distinguished:

1. **Supply-oriented transport strategies.** Examples are:
   - improvement of public transport (for instance in combination with deregulation as in Manchester, or combined use of regional railway network by urban tramway in Karlsruhe);

- more efficient management and organization of transport systems technology;
- design of sophisticated new infrastructures (light rail, subterranean solutions and so on);
- incentives for using telematics in transport systems;
- parking policy (in terms of volume, location and opening hours).

2. **Non-transport strategies.** Examples are:
   - alternative work schedules to avoid transport peak problems (analogous to electricity load management);
   - further introduction of telecommunication to favour telework, teleshopping, etc;
   - urban design, urban land use and urban street design (such as building permits for new offices near terminals of public transport in the Netherlands).

A considerable part of urban traffic problems is caused by rigid location patterns of buildings, facilities and infrastructures and hence cannot easily be removed in the short run. However, from a strategic viewpoint, various long-term options may be considered such as the construction of compact residential buildings in the vicinity of accessible public transport stations.

MARKETING

Urban energy planning objectives must be accompanied by well thought out marketing strategies and investment plans of local utilities. For instance, there may be a blend of physical urban planning and energy planning, in which local space heating supply systems may favour urban quality of life as a major goal of urban sustainability policy. Similarly, the substitution of conventional oil- or coal-based space heating for more environment-friendly alternatives (for example natural gas and cogenerated district heating) may reduce the ambient concentration of pollutants. This would, through a reduction of social costs of energy provision, increase the overall energy efficiency, as examples from various European countries have shown. The promotion of more sustainable energy policies at the urban level should of course highlight the benefits of more efficient urban energy plans, but should also emphasize the likelihood of implementing such urban energy systems in practice. Only in this case will there be a general acceptance of new institutional configurations, in which energy utility companies may act as energy service companies. Clearly, cities may – temporarily – support the development of such energy service companies by providing financial assistance during the initial phase (and - whenever possible - by using their influence on the marketing and investment strategies of publicly-owned energy utility companies). A critical judgement of existing experiences and the sharing of information on successful cases in a European context would then be desirable. Unfortunately, focused marketing of urban energy and environmental policies is still very rare, and should increasingly be encouraged in order to increase the potential of such policies. Creating a network of European cities in which information on promising policy actions (or on new scientific research) can be transferred to a broad set of European cities (and agencies therein) is also very beneficial. Maximizing the total social benefits of urban environmental and energy policies requires institutional adjustments by agencies and all other players involved in urban energy and environmental policy. Also at the European level a closer mutual focus of energy, regional and environmental policies would be highly desirable.

INFORMATION TRANSFER

Different cities vary enormously; and there is also a great diversity in urban energy and environmental policies. There are based on, for example, solar heating, peak load management, geothermal sources combined heat power systems, and so on. A system of disseminating appropriate information and know-how on such initiatives would be extremely helpful for increasing energy efficiency in various cities in the European Community, especially if combined with complementary indicators such as ecological quality, emission of pollutants (SO_2, NO_x, CO_2 etc). Systematic urban energy impact analysis and well-structured decision support methods may be particularly useful here, especially since a quick transfer of relevant knowledge may contribute to preventive environmental policies. Various experiences described in this book point out the potential of such new endeavours, especially if they are combined with decentralized information provision or information centres. Besides, in this context exchange of expert knowledge and training of experts may also be an important vehicle. A broader policy programme, then, focusing on a wide range of services rendered to local energy initiatives is desirable. Examples are information provision, problem diagnosis, assistance and consultation programmes, demonstration projects of local energy projects, etc. It goes without saying that all such new endeavours would have to be based on proper urban energy information and monitoring systems (using amongst other things remote controls, remote alarms and remote measurements) that also incorporate relevant sectoral, spatial and environmental information.

TOWARDS A EUROPEAN URBAN ENERGY PROGRAMME?

The case studies reported in this book show the potential benefits of appropriate urban energy and environmental plans. Instead of straightforward energy capacity expansion (with all environmental externalities involved) alternative options *do* exist through clever management and the rearrangement of existing options. However, information on good case studies is rare. What is primarily needed is essentially a cross-European programme on urban energy planning that serves to disseminate information on successful and innovative urban energy policies. 'Success stories' of urban energy policy will provide new insights for other European cities, and are therefore of paramount importance, in particular because at present the communications between cities are undoubtedly unsatisfactory. This information needs to be collected on a systematic basis. Such well-focused cross-European urban energy initiatives might provide a stimulus and a catalyst for new ways of energy planning in Europe.

Urban energy planning is a potentially promising field which deserves further exploration on the basis of illustrative demonstration projects and pilot studies. Special attention would have to be given to:

- institutional arrangements regarding urban energy planning;
- third-party financing schemes in an urban context;
- bottlenecks in urban district heating and cogeneration plans;
- longitudinal urban energy auditing and monitoring schemes;
- R&D efforts necessary for a mature urban energy planning;
- the relevance of urban energy planning as part of the flanking policies in the context of the Structural Funds of the European Community.

The road towards sustainable cities in Europe will not be an easy one, but it may be expected that intensive and creative initiatives – translated into effective policy measures – will form the cornerstones of such a sustainability-oriented urban system.

In conclusion, cities can act as catalysts in rationalizing energy–environmental policy in Europe. Such a role is beneficial for both our planet as a whole and for the individual cities in particular. Efficient and effective urban energy and environmental policy will not only enhance urban sustainability, but it will also renew the fabric and infrastructure of the towns and cities of Europe.

REFERENCES

Allaert, C, C Rul, and M Rosier (1980) *Warmtekaart van Belgie* Final Report, Dept. of Physical Planning, State University, Gent (mimeographed)

Archibugi, F, and P Nijkamp (eds) (1990) *Economy and Ecology. Towards Sustainable Development* Kluwer, Dordrecht

Banister, D, and K Button (eds) (1993) *Transport, the Environment and Sustainable Development* E&F Spon, London

Becht, H Y, and G J Zijlstra (1985) 'Zuid-Holland kan Miljarden Investeren in Warmte/Kracht' *Energiebeheer*, no 11, pp 26–31

Bergh, J C J M van den (1991) *Dynamic Models for Sustainable Development* Thesis Publishers, Amsterdam

Berry, B J L (1974) *Land Use, Urban Form and Environmental Quality* University of Chicago, Chicago

Berry, R, (1985) 'Islands of Renewal in Seas of Decay' *The New Urban Reality* (P Peterson, ed) The Brookings Institution, Washington, DC, pp 123-140

Blair, P (1979) *Multiobjective Regional Energy Planning* Martinus Nijhoff, Boston/The Hague

Breheney, M (ed) (1992) *Sustainable Development and Urban Form*, Pion, London

Brouwer, F M (1987) *Integrated Environmental Modelling* Kluwer, Dordrecht

Cecchini, P (1989) *The European Challenge 1992* Gower, Aldershot, UK

Chateau, B, and B Lapillone (1979) 'Long-term Energy Demand Simulations' *Energy Models for the EC* (A Strub, ed) European Community, Directorate-General XVII, Brussels, pp 120-128

Chatterji, M (1980) 'Energy Modeling with Particular Reference to Spatial Systems' *Regional Science and Urban Economics*, vol 10, pp 325–342

Costanza, R (1975) *The Spatial Distribution of Land Use Subsystems, Incoming Energy and Energy Use* MS Thesis, Department of Ecology, University of Florida, Gainesville, Florida

Davelaar, E J and P Nijkamp (1989) 'Spatial Dispersion of Technological Innovation' *Journal of Regional Science* vol 29, no 3, pp 325–346

EC (1991) *Energy and Urban Environment* DG XVII, Brussels

Elkin, T, D Maclaren, and M Hillman (1990) *Reviving the City: Towards Sustainable Urban Development* Policy Studies Institute, London

Fischer, M, and P Nijkamp (eds) (1993) *Geographic Information Systems, Spatial Modelling and Policy Evaluation* Springer Berlin

Foell, W K (1980) 'A Systems Approach to Regional Energy/Environment Management' *Regional Science and Urban Economics* vol 10, pp 303–24

Giaoutzi, M, and P Nijkamp (1993) *Decision Support Models for Regional Sustainable Development* Avebury, Aldershot, UK

Guldmann, J-M (1983) 'Modelling the Structure of Gas Distribution Costs in Urban Areas' *Regional Science and Urban Economics* vol 13, no 3, pp 299–316

Guldmann, J-M (1984) 'Economies of Scale and Natural Monopoly in Urban Utilities' *Geographical Analysis* vol 17, no 4, pp 302–317

Guldmann, J-M (1985) 'An Econometric Model of Electricity Distribution Systems in Urban Areas' *Environment & Planning A* vol 16, pp 793–806

Haefele, W (1982) *Energy in a Finite World* Ballinger, Cambridge

Hafkamp, W (1986) *Economic–Environmental Modeling in a Multiregional System* North-Holland Publ Co, Amsterdam

Helm, D, and F McGowan (1987) 'European Lessons for the Privatisation of the UK Electricity Supply Industry' *ENER Bulletin*, October, no 3, pp 9–20

Hirst, E (1987) 'Electric Utility Energy Conservation and Load Management Programmes' *Energy Policy*, April, pp 103–108

Hordijk, L (1991) *An Integrated Assessment Model for Acidification in Europe* PhD Thesis, Free University, Amsterdam

Hudson, E A, and D W Jorgenson (1976) 'Tax Policy and Energy Conservation' *Econometric Studies of US Energy Policy* (D W Jorgenson, ed), North-Holland Publ Co, Amsterdam, pp 9–94

Hutchinson, D (1991) 'Co-generation and Sustainability', Paper, Conference British Regional Science Association, Oxford

IEA (International Energy Agency) (1986) *Energy for Buildings*, OECD, Paris

IEA (International Energy Agency) (1987) *Energy Conservation in IEA Countries*, OECD, Paris

IEA (International Energy Agency). (1988) *Energy Policies and Programmes in IEA Countries* OECD, Paris

InnoTec (1986) *Regionale Energiefluszanalyse Berlin*, Report, Berlin (mimeographed)

Johansson, B, and T R Lakshmanan (1985) *Regional Impacts of Large Scale Energy Development* North-Holland Publishing Co, Amsterdam

Jorgenson, D W (ed) (1976) *Econometric Studies of US Energy Policy* North-Holland Publishing Co, Amsterdam

Juul, K and P Nijkamp (eds) (1989) *Urban Energy Planning*, DG XVII, EC, Brussels

Karkkainen, S, V Kekkonen, and A Ranne (1982) 'Simulation and Optimization Models in the Expansion Planning Studies of District Heating Systems', Paper 5th International District Heating Conference, September, Kiev, USSR (mimeographed)

Laconte, P, J Gibson, and A Rapoport (eds) (1982) *Human and Energy Factors in Urban Planning: A Systems Approach* Martinus Nijhoff, The Hague

Lakshmanan, T R, and P Nijkamp (eds) (1980) *Energy–Environmental Analysis* Gower, Aldershot

Lovelock, J (1979) *Gaia: A New Look at Life on Earth* Oxford University Press, Oxford

Lesuis, P, F Muller, and P Nijkamp (1980) 'An Interregional Policy Model for Energy–Economic–Environmental Interactions' *Regional Science and Urban Economics* vol 10, pp 343–70

MacKerron, G (ed) (1989) *Regional Energy* DG XVII, Commission of the European Communities, Brussels

Marahrens, W, Chr Ax, and G Buck (eds) (1991) *Stadt und Umwelt* Birkhäuser, Basel

Muller, F (1979) *Energy and Environment in Interregional Input-Output Models* Martinus Nijhoff, Boston/The Hague

Newman, P W G, and J R Kenworthy (1992) 'Is There a Role for Physical Planners' *Journal of the American Planning Association* vol 58, pp 353–362

Nijkamp, P (ed) (1990) *Urban Sustainability* Gower, Avebury

Nijkamp, P (1983) 'Regional Dimensions of Energy Scarcity' *Environment and Planning C: Government and Policy*, vol 1, no 2, pp 179–92

Nijkamp, P (1985) 'Regional Information Systems and Impact Analysis for Large-Scale Energy Developments' *Large-Scale Energy Projects* (T R Lakshmanan and B Johansson, eds), Elsevier, Amsterdam, pp 257–272

Nijkamp, P, and A Reggiani (1992) *Interaction, Evolution and Chaos in Space* Springer-Verlag, Berlin

Nijkamp, P, and D Tiemersma (1985) 'Spatially-oriented Energy Consumption Scenarios' *Geographical Dimensions of Energy* (F J Calzonetti and B D Salomon, eds), Reidel, Dordrecht, pp 299–323

Nijkamp, P, and A Volwahsen (1990) 'New Directions in Integrated Regional Energy Planning' *Energy Policy* pp 764–774

Odum, E P (1976) *Ecology* Holt, Rinehart and Winston, London

OECD (1978) *Urban Environmental Indicators* Paris

Oortmarssen, G J, van (1987) 'De Acceptatie door Huishoudens van het Afschakelen van Wasmachines tijdens Piekuren door een Electriciteitsbedrijf' IVAM-UvA, Amsterdam

Orishimo, I (1982) *Urbanisation and Environmental Quality* Kluwer, Dordrecht

Owens, S E (1992) 'Land-Use Planning for Energy Efficiency' *Applied Energy* vol 43, pp 81–114

Pearce, D, A Markandaya, and E B Barbier (1989) *Blueprint for a Green Economy* Earthscan, London

Perrels, A, and P Nijkamp (1988) 'Energy Demand in a Long-Term Perspective; Possible Implications of Time Scheduling' Research Memorandum 1987-60, Faculty of Economics, Free University, Amsterdam

Rath-Nagel, S (1987) *Guidebook on Regional Energy Planning* Report, GOPA-Consultants, Bad Homburg

Ratick, S, and T R Lakshmanan (1983) 'An Overview of the Strategic Environmental Assessment System', *Systems and Models for Energy and Environmental Analysis* (T R Lakshmanan and P Nijkamp, eds) Gower, Aldershot, pp 126–52

Rickaby, P A (1991) 'Energy and Urban Development in an Archetypical English Town' *Environment and Planning B*, Vol 18, pp 153–176

Rogner, H H (1984) *Dynamic Energy Complex Analysis for Metropolitan Regions* Report, IIASA, Laxenburg

Rüdig, W (1986) 'Energy Conservation and Electricity Utilities' *Energy Policy*, April, pp 104–116

Sassin, W (1982) 'Urbanisation and the Global Energy Problem' *Human and Energy Factors in Urban Planning: A Systems Approach* (P Laconte, L Gibson and W Rappoport, eds) Martinus Nijhoff, The Hague

Schieke, W E (1987) 'Loadmanagement in de Praktijk' *Energieconsulent*, no 5, pp 16–18

Sexton, R J, N Brown Johnson, and A Konakayama (1987) 'Consumer Response to Continuous-display Electricity-use Monitors in a Time-of-use Pricing Experiment' *Journal of Consumer Research*, vol 14, 1987, pp 55–61.

Solomon, A P (ed) *The Prospective City: Economic, Population, Energy and Environmental Development* MIT Press, Cambridge, 1980

Stren, R E (1992) *Sustainable Cities* Westview Press, Boulder

Thabit, S S, and J Stark (1985) 'Decentralized Energy Supply' *Energy Policy*, pp 71–83

Train, K E, D L McFadden, and A A Goett (1987) 'Consumer Attitudes and Voluntary Rate Schedules for Public Utilities' *The Review of Economics and Statistics* vol 69, no 3, pp 383–391

UNEP (1993) *Urban Air Pollution in Mega-Cities of the World* Basil Blackwell, Oxford

Verbruggen, A, and C Buyse (1986) 'Industrial Configuration and its Costs Duplications for Centralised Electricity Supply' *Proceedings of Gas and Electricity Conference* Benelux Association of Energy Economists, pp 399–416

WAES (1976) *Energy Demand Studies* MIT Press, Cambridge, Mass

Ward, B (1976) *The Home of Man* Norton, New York

WCED (1987) *Our Common Future* Oxford University Press, Oxford

Webster, F V, Ph Bly and N J Paulley (eds) (1988) *Urban Land-use and Transport Interaction* Avebury, Aldershot

Wegener, M, Mackett, R L, and D C Simmonds (1991) 'One City, Three Models: Comparison of Land-Use/Transport Policy Simulation Models for Dortmund' *Transport Reviews*, vol 11, pp 107–129

Wene, C O (1987) 'Using a Comprehensive Model for Municipal Energy Planning, Report, Energy Systems Technology' Chalmers University of Technology, Gothenburg (mimeographed)